RUN TO THE BROKENNESS

Copyright © 2025 by Kevin Foster

Published by AVAIL

All rights reserved. No portion of this book may be reproduced, stored in a retrieval system, or transmitted in any form or by any means—electronic, mechanical, photocopy, recording, scanning, or other—except for brief quotations in critical reviews or articles, without prior written permission of the author.

Unless otherwise specified, all Scripture quotations are taken from the Holy Bible, New International Version®, NIV®. Copyright © 1973, 1978, 1984, 2011 by Biblica, Inc.™ Used by permission of Zondervan. All rights reserved worldwide. www.zondervan.com. The "NIV" and "New International Version" are trademarks registered in the United States Patent and Trademark Office by Biblica, Inc.™ | Scripture quotations marked BSB are from The Holy Bible, Berean Study Bible, BSB, Copyright ©2016, 2020 by Bible Hub Used by Permission. All Rights Reserved Worldwide. | Scripture quotations marked ESV are from The ESV® Bible (The Holy Bible, English Standard Version®), copyright © 2001 by Crossway, a publishing ministry of Good News Publishers. Used by permission. All rights reserved. | Scripture quotations marked KJV are taken from the King James Version of the Bible. Public domain. | Scripture quotations marked MSG are taken from THE MESSAGE, copyright © 1993, 1994, 1995, 1996, 2000, 2001, 2002 by Eugene H. Peterson. Used by permission of NavPress. All rights reserved. Represented by Tyndale House Publishers, Inc. | Scripture quotations marked NKJV are taken from the New King James Version®. Copyright © 1982 by Thomas Nelson. Used by permission. All rights reserved. | Scripture quotations marked NLT are taken from the Holy Bible, New Living Translation, copyright © 1996, 2004, 2015 by Tyndale House Foundation. Used by permission of Tyndale House Publishers, Inc., Carol Stream, Illinois 60188. All rights reserved.

For foreign and subsidiary rights, contact the author.

Cover design by: Sara Young
Cover photo by: Andrew van Tilborgh

ISBN: 978-1-964794-92-1   1 2 3 4 5 6 7 8 9 10

Printed in the United States of America

RUN TO THE BROKENNESS

HOW YOUR CHURCH CAN BE THE CENTER OF YOUR COMMUNITY

KEVIN FOSTER

WHAT PEOPLE ARE SAYING ABOUT
RUN TO THE BROKENNESS

First responders are my heroes. They run to the fire, the chaos, the disaster—often to life-altering brokenness. I've had car accidents and health challenges, so my experiences have filled me with appreciation. In his book, *Run to the Brokenness*, my friend Kevin Foster will take you on a very personal and real journey and invite you to opportunities in your own communities to become first responders. This book is not just for churches, but businesses, communities, and individuals. This book is for anyone who wants to live a life that would make an exceptional difference in someone's life.

—SAM CHAND
Leadership Consultant
Author of *Leadership Pain*

Not only have I had the joy of knowing Kevin Foster as a friend but also the privilege of watching him grow as a pastor and leader for over fourteen years. His heart for people, his willingness to engage brokenness head-on, and his vision for the local church are not just theory—they're lived out in the trenches. In *Run to the Brokenness,* Kevin issues a powerful call for churches to become centers of hope, healing, and transformation. This book is more than inspiration—it's a roadmap, forged in prayer, service, and real, hard-fought and hard-won experience. I highly recommend *Run to the Brokenness* to any pastor as a transformational resource, to move beyond walls and into the heart of the community.

—RICH GUERRA
SoCal Network Superintendent, Assemblies of God

As mayor of Fresno, one of California's largest and most diverse cities, I've seen firsthand how faith-based organizations can play a vital role in strengthening communities. Under Kevin Foster's leadership, LifeBridge Community Church has become more than a place of worship; it's become a hub of compassion, innovation, and transformation. *Run to the Brokenness* offers a practical and inspiring roadmap for how churches can serve their cities holistically. Every civic leader should hope to have a church like LifeBridge in their community.

—**MAYOR JERRY DYER**
Fresno, CA

During his days as a student at North Central University, I found Kevin to be a caring person with a heart for all kinds of people. This heart of his still beats strong for service to those who need it most. You need to read *Run to the Brokenness*. It will take you outside of yourself and motivate you to step up your compassion index. The book is easy to read, practical in application, and full of stories showing the grace and mercy of God. You'll be challenged to view your church as a hub of the community to bring healing and hope. Don't miss this one!

—**DR. CAROLYN TENNANT**
Speaker and author
University VP and professor at NCU and AGTS

In *Run to the Brokenness*, Kevin Foster offers more than inspiration—he offers a model. As someone who works nationally with faith-based organizations, I've seen firsthand how rare it is to find a church that is spiritually dynamic *and* socially impactful. Kevin's leadership through LifeBridge and the ACTS Foundation has helped secure significant grant funding, not just for his church, but for dozens of others. This book will challenge and equip any leader who wants to create lasting community change.

—**SCOTT WEAD**
The National Grant Center

Run to the Brokenness is a crucial book for such a time as this. The twin disruptions of COVID and unprecedented political chaos have relegated the twentieth-century ministry model to the dustbin of history. Doing church like it's 1995 will no longer get the job done. Savvy leaders recognize we've got to pivot to a new normal, but the future church feels like uncharted territory. *Run to the Brokenness* provides a biblically sound, real-world tested, and principle-based framework for leading your church toward effective ministry in a twenty-first-century world. No theories conjured up in an ivory tower. Kevin transparently shares the joys, sorrows, and setbacks he's journeyed through to discover the way forward.

—STEVE PIKE
Founder, Next Wave Community
NextWave.Community

In a world marked by pain and brokenness, *Run to the Brokenness* is a compelling call to action for the local church. Pastor Kevin—a friend and devoted leader at LifeBridge Church in Fresno, California—beautifully articulates the Church's vital role in embodying the healing presence of Christ in our communities. Having pastored in the same city for decades, I've learned that people rarely seek true help when life seems perfect. Rather, it's in their struggles that they open their hearts. Jesus reminds us, "Don't say, 'Four months more, and then the harvest.' I tell you, open your eyes and look at the fields! They are ripe for harvest now." The Church must recognize that the ripe harvest is, in fact, the broken and hurting all around us.

Some may believe the government is capable of healing society's deepest wounds, but we must understand its limitations. While government can offer aid, it cannot speak the transformative truth of the gospel. That sacred responsibility has been entrusted to the Church. Real healing in our communities requires changed hearts and renewed minds—and only the gospel can bring that transformation. Pastor Kevin's insights powerfully reaffirm that the local church—on every street, in every neighborhood—is God's chosen infrastructure for healing. As Jesus declared, "I will build my Church, and the gates of Hell will not prevail against it." *Run to the Brokenness* will challenge and inspire you to see the greatest needs in your community not as problems to avoid, but as invitations to the most meaningful Kingdom work your church will ever undertake. This book is more than a guide—it's a call to join God in His healing mission to the world.

—WENDELL VINSON
Pastor of Canyon Hills Church
President and Cofounder of CityServe

I love it when I see books that chase after the very heart of God. Through his new book, *Run to the Brokenness*, Kevin gives you the blueprint of how you and your church can find purpose and meaning through meeting the needs of those who need it most. The broken, forgotten, and overlooked are those whom God chases after. When your church chases after what God chases, God will chase after you! I'm so glad this much-needed book has been written for leaders and churches around the world. I know once you read it, it will change your perspective on what's important and bring hope and life to those you touch.

—CRAIG JOHNSON
Associate Pastor, Lakewood Church
Founder of Champions Clubs

But what if the local church could impact not just someone's eternity, which is of utmost importance—but also their social and economic well-being? Kevin Foster asks the important questions in his new book, *Run to the Brokenness*. Jesus gives us the model in which to serve and love our neighbors, and the truth is that our neighbors are hurting and broken. It's too easy to be distracted by metrics and measurables of running a church as an organization, keeping our focus inward. Kevin reminds us of the importance of being the hands and feet of Jesus in practical ways, constantly pushing our focus outward. As he says, "Now is the time. Let's go!"

—NICKY STADE
Executive Director of Women of SoCal, SoCal Network
Associate Pastor, RefugeOC, Orange, CA

Dedication

To Ellen . . . Your quiet strength, unwavering love, and belief in the calling on my life have been my anchor. You are the greatest gift God has given me.

To my daughters: Cara, Brynn, and Laney. . . Thank you for your patience, your grace, and your unwavering support through the long days and late nights of building a church that serves as a hub for our community. You've grown up in the middle of the mission, and yet you've never resented the weight of it; you've embraced it. I'm proud of the way you love God deeply and authentically. I'm even more proud of how you love people and how you love our church. You serve with joy, lead with integrity, and carry the heart of this house in everything you do. This book and this vision exist because of sacrifices you've made. I pray the legacy we're building is one you're proud to carry forward.

And to LifeBridge Community Church . . . You are the living example that the Church can run to the brokenness. Thank you for embodying the heart of this book long before it was ever written.

CONTENTS

Foreword... *xiii*

Acknowledgments...................................*xv*

Introduction 17

CHAPTER 1. RETHINKING SUCCESS IN THE LOCAL CHURCH.... 23

CHAPTER 2. CHANGE THE METRICS................. 51

CHAPTER 3. IDENTIFY THE NEED 75

CHAPTER 4. RESPOND TO COMMUNITY CRISIS........... 95

CHAPTER 5. BROKENNESS IS AN OPPORTUNITY 111

CHAPTER 6. CREATING THE RIGHT CULTURE 119

CHAPTER 7. PASSION FOR YOUR COMMUNITY 139

CHAPTER 8. FUNDING THE MISSION 151

CHAPTER 9. OCCUPATIONAL HAZARDS OF MINISTRY.......167

CHAPTER 10. YOU CAN CHANGE YOUR COMMUNITY.........185

FOREWORD

When I speak at conferences, I often ask the audience to raise their hands if they are a lead pastor at a church. Inevitably, several hands go up to acknowledge their leadership position. I then ask the question, "How many of you pastor a city?" The hands quickly go up out of pure reflex but then quickly come down when they begin to process the question. It is then that the awkward moment happens: when lead pastors in the room begin to question whether they are simply pastoring a church or if they are pastoring a city.

This concept, unfortunately, can be foreign to leaders. The belief that we are only to lead the churches God has entrusted us, but that we are also to be leaders and influencers of the city. We need to meet needs and provide leadership in the communities where our churches reside in such a powerful way that even the non-believing leaders in our city would shudder at the thought of our churches closing their doors.

Run to the Brokenness hits this topic straight on in a practical and realistic way. It is one of those books that cuts through the noise and presents a clear vision of what the church can and should be. Authored by my friend Kevin Foster, this book will move you and your team into the place of influence God is leading us all, to pastor not only our churches but our cities.

As the founder of South Hills Church in Southern California and Church BOOM, a coaching network committed to resourcing pastors across America, I've spent my life helping church leaders move from stuck to thriving. I've coached hundreds of pastors through the unique challenges of ministry, and I can tell you, what Kevin writes here isn't theory. It's not recycled ideas. It's the hard-won wisdom of a pastor who has lived the pain, embraced the call, and now leads one of the most community-integrated churches I've ever seen.

Kevin Foster is the real deal. His work through LifeBridge Community Church and the ACTS Foundation in Fresno, CA, is a national model for what it means to be a church that serves spiritually, socially, and economically. His story will resonate with pastors who feel the weight of leading in today's world, and his strategy will offer practical hope for churches that want to matter Monday through Saturday, not just on Sunday.

—Chris Sonksen
Founder of South Hills Church and Church BOOM

ACKNOWLEDGMENTS

This book would not exist without the grace of God and the people He's placed in my life to guide, challenge, and encourage me.

To Rich Guerra—thank you for consistently pushing me to write this book and for being a shining example of what it looks like to lead churches with a heart for the broken. Your leadership has inspired and shaped this message deeply.

To Gary Grogan, aka PapaG—from the time I interned under you in 1995 to the years I served on your staff, your example has never left me. You showed me firsthand what it means to lead a church that runs to the brokenness.

To Chris Sonksen—thank you for challenging me to finish the book. Your words sparked the momentum I needed to cross the line.

To Gary Zelesky—thank you for your patient, prophetic coaching. You didn't just help me write; you helped call the gift out of me. I am a better communicator because of your investment.

RUN TO THE BROKENNESS

To every pastor and leader who's ever questioned whether their church could really make a difference—this book is for you. May it give you hope, strategy, and courage to run boldly toward the broken places.

INTRODUCTION

Your church can be the hub, the center, of your neighborhood and community by running to the brokenness. Regardless of your Sunday attendance numbers, your church can become one of the most influential organizations in your city. As culture drifts further from the local church, one of the most powerful ways to become relevant again is to engage with the brokenness in the community around you.

This book is here to inspire you, not just to believe that you can make a difference but that you already are, and that your impact can grow beyond anything you imagined, no matter the size of your church or your budget.

God has equipped you and your congregation with a unique voice, presence, and purpose—one that no other church in your area can fulfill. And if you're like me, there are days when it's hard to see that clearly. Sometimes, the only thing I feel I can measure is how many people are in the seats or how much is left in the church's checking account. When the sanctuary is full, I feel like I can take on the world. But when it's empty, when everyone's at the coast or in the mountains, I feel like giving up.

WHAT IF WE CHANGED THE METRICS?

What if we measured impact not just on Sundays, but Monday through Saturday?

Right now, over 40 percent of pastors are seriously considering leaving full-time ministry.[1] Many of us are carrying the weight of discouragement, burnout, and unmet expectations. Could it be that we're measuring the wrong things?

If success is only tied to how many show up on Sunday, no wonder we're exhausted. And no wonder our communities are still waiting for help.

But what if the local church could impact not just someone's eternity—which is of utmost importance—but also their social and economic well-being?

Imagine this: a jobless person from your city walks into your church. They receive Christ. They receive food and clothes for their family. They get connected to job training. Eventually, they secure a job with a livable wage. All because *your church showed up.*

This is possible. It happens regularly for us. And it can happen regularly for you too.

I believe that the measure of success for the local church must shift—from how many people attend to how well the people of the church are running to the brokenness that surrounds it. When that shift happens, your church will gain an influence that transcends Sunday morning.

What if the people in your community viewed your church as being just as important as the fire department or police

---

[1] Barna, "Pastors Share Top Reasons They've Considered Quitting Ministry in the Past Year," 27 Apr. 2022, https://www.barna.com/research/pastors-quitting-ministry/.

INTRODUCTION

station? I'm so grateful for our first responders. They're there when people need them most. That's what we wanted our church to be: a place people could count on when life fell apart.

One of those moments came during my daughter Brynn's seventh-grade year. It was her first year walking to the bus stop without my wife driving her. On Friday, November 3, 2017, I was at a tire shop getting quotes when my wife called. I'll never forget the fear in her voice.

She told me that Brynn had just shared something terrifying: that morning, a man in a black SUV had tried to abduct her.

Brynn had seen the SUV pull into the neighborhood. Something didn't feel right. The man rolled down his window and offered her a ride, but she said no and kept walking. He circled around, cut her off at the next intersection, and this time shouted: "GET IN THE CAR NOW!"

Brynn ran toward the bus stop where other students were waiting.

She was too scared to tell anyone at school. When Ellen and I found out, we called the police. Officers came and began knocking on neighbors' doors to check for video footage. The very last house they tried had a camera pointed directly at the spot where it happened.

Our neighbor invited us in and showed us the footage, which matched Brynn's story exactly. The black SUV. The man's voice. Brynn running away. Watching it was heartbreaking. I couldn't stop thinking, *If he had gotten her into that car. . . .*

This moment could have altered my daughter's life forever.

Thankfully, we had proof. The news covered the story that night, and through tears, I was able to share our faith in Jesus and how we pray daily for our children's protection.

It was a terrifying experience, but it opened the door for a testimony. It reminded me how thankful I was that the police were there for my family.

And it raised powerful questions:

What if people viewed your church as the hub they can trust and run to with the same kind of urgent needs?

What if people in your community felt YOUR church was just as important as the first responders in your city?

I'm not just talking about people who already attend. I'm talking about the *average* person, the unchurched, the skeptical, and the broken, who couldn't care less about God or your Sunday service. What if even they freaked out in the same manner if they knew your church was going to close as they would if the local fire department closed? It's possible to become that relevant!

When my wife and I moved to Fresno, California, on August 1, 2004, we had no building, no funding, no launch team—just a dream.

We were what's called a "parachute church plant." We moved across the country from Illinois, leaving behind a church we loved and had revitalized. We had no salary, no safety net, just a beat-up U-Haul and a vision from God to build a church that would become a true center point of the community. A church that would be viewed on the same level of importance as the first responders.

INTRODUCTION

We had no connections in Fresno. We were Midwesterners who felt like strangers in a foreign land. But we had a calling. And that calling carried us across states, through exhaustion, and into a brand-new beginning.

If you're reading this and feel like *your* vision seems impossible—you're not alone.

My prayer is that this book will inspire you to keep going, challenge you to rethink success, and equip you with the mindset and tools you need to run to the brokenness in your own backyard.

Because if God can use me, He can use you.

Let's go.

CHAPTER 1

RETHINKING SUCCESS IN THE LOCAL CHURCH

I believe the philosophy that now drives our ministry—running to the brokenness and impacting people spiritually, socially, and economically—was born when I was just a kid.

I grew up on the "wrong side of town," the son of a hard-working, blue-collar father who spent most of his career working for Chrysler Corporation. In the early 1980s, the American auto industry was in crisis. The economy was struggling, layoffs were common, and families like mine were hit especially hard.

I remember seasons when my dad was laid off from the plant, and dinner for our family of five was nothing more than bean soup for weeks at a time. When the plant work wasn't enough to sustain us, he'd take a second job cleaning buildings at night. He would come home exhausted from the factory, catch a few hours of sleep, and then head out again just to keep food on the table and the lights on.

Even in that season of struggle, I saw something that would shape my view of ministry for life.

There was a man in our neighborhood, homeless, hungry, and living on the streets. I still remember the day my mom invited him into our home. At first, my siblings and I were nervous. We didn't know his story or what to expect. But over time, we came to know him. He wasn't scary; he was human, just like us. And in many ways, he was broken; just like we were.

We didn't have much. But my mom taught me this: when you have Jesus, you always have enough to share.

Looking back now, I realize she was modeling something that I would later build my entire ministry around. She wasn't just feeding a man; she was restoring dignity. She was running to the brokenness.

And that's the heartbeat of this book. What if our churches did what my mom did? What if, instead of pulling away from the broken, we moved toward them? What if our churches were known not for how many people we seat on Sundays but for how many people we serve Monday through Saturday?

That vision was born in my childhood home, and I've been chasing it ever since.

So, what would it look like if your church embodied that same spirit of selfless, inconvenient love? It's the kind of question that demands more than a passing thought—it calls for shifting your perspective and responding to the challenge to think differently about your local church.

If you've been a pastor or church leader for any length of time, you know the unspoken pressure we all feel: to measure our success by how many people are in the building on

Sunday morning. We want full sanctuaries, packed pews, and growing attendance. But here's the reality—only 21 percent of Americans now attend religious services weekly, with another 9 percent attending almost every week. That means nearly three out of four Americans are not regularly gathering on Sundays. In fact, 56 percent of Americans say they seldom or never attend church, and this trend is especially pronounced among younger generations. [2] The reasons vary—disillusionment with institutions, shifting cultural norms, or a simple lack of connection between Sunday gatherings and everyday life.

So, what if we changed the standard?

What if we moved beyond Sunday morning attendance as the primary metric of success?

What if we redefined what it means to be an effective, fruitful, and faithful church?

We'll explore this more deeply in chapter 2, but for now, consider this:

What if success in the local church wasn't measured only by how many people gather on Sunday, but by how many lives are being transformed Monday through Saturday?

What if the success of your church was measured by how well it runs to the brokenness in your community?

What if we expanded our metrics, not replacing the spiritual (which is most important), but complementing it with the social and economic well-being of the people we serve? Think food, clothing, shelter, the basic needs at the foundation of

---

2 Jeffrey M. Jones, "Church Attendance Has Declined in Most U.S. Religious Groups," *Gallup*, 25 Mar. 2024, https://news.gallup.com/poll/642548/church-attendance-declined-religious-groups.aspx.

RUN TO THE BROKENNESS

Maslow's hierarchy. Psychologist Abraham Maslow proposed that human beings have a progression of needs, starting with the most basic physiological needs (like food, water, and shelter), followed by safety, belonging, esteem, and finally, self-actualization. In ministry, we often aim for spiritual transformation (which aligns with the highest levels of the hierarchy), but we must not overlook the foundational needs because if someone is hungry or homeless, it's much harder for them to receive the deeper truths of the gospel. Meeting these practical needs creates the conditions where spiritual growth can truly take root.

What if someone was able to secure a job because of your church? What if someone underemployed was able to pick up a side job because your church created that opportunity? What if someone had a roof over their head today because your church stepped in when no one else did?

It's possible. And this book will show you how.

Let me be clear: this book is not anti-growth, anti-Sunday, or anti-large, anti-small, or anti-medium church. I've learned from and served alongside many thriving large churches doing extraordinary work. In fact, many of them *are* already running to the brokenness in their cities, leading the way in compassion, outreach, and innovation.

But I also know that most churches in America are small. Research shows that 59 percent of churches have fewer than one hundred people in weekly attendance, and the median church size in North America is just sixty-five attendees.[3]

---

3 Emma Davis, "30 Church Trends You Need to Know for 2024," *Reach Right*, 3 Jan. 2024, https://reachrightstudios.com/blog/church-statistics-2024/.

MINISTRY SUCCESS ISN'T A FORMULA TO MASTER; IT'S A MYSTERY TO STEWARD.

The heart of this book is to affirm and equip every type of church—large, small, urban, rural, growing, plateaued, revitalizing, or replanting—to embrace its God-given opportunity, to become the center of its community by running boldly to the brokenness that surrounds it.

WHY YOUR CHURCH MATTERS

Jesus said in Matthew 16:18, "And I tell you that you are Peter, and on this rock I will build my church, and the gates of Hades will not overcome it."

Two timeless truths from this passage form the foundation of your local church:

1) **Jesus is the One who builds.**

The church is not ultimately built by our talents, strategies, or even our dedication—it is built by Jesus Himself. He says, "I will build My church." The pressure of growth does not rest solely on our shoulders. This truth should bring peace to every pastor and ministry leader: while we are called to labor faithfully, it is Christ who does the supernatural work.

Church work is unlike any other profession. In most fields, hard work and diligence almost always produce visible, measurable results. But in ministry, the results don't always correlate directly to our effort. I know many faithful servants who work tirelessly, love deeply, and lead with excellence, yet they don't always see the numeric growth they desire.

This isn't a call to laziness or resignation; we should absolutely do everything possible to build healthy, thriving ministries. However, even after doing all the "right things," the outcome remains in God's hands. It's His church. It's a divine partnership: 100 percent God and 100 percent us.

Ministry success isn't a formula to master; it's a mystery to steward. Growth, whether numerical, spiritual, or relational is ultimately something only God can produce.

2) The gates of hell will not prevail against your church.

Hell itself, all the forces of darkness, cannot stop what Jesus is building. Satan's attacks are real, and opposition is guaranteed, but Jesus's victory is even more real and far greater.

This means that when you feel the most discouraged, when obstacles seem insurmountable, and when it feels like nothing is moving forward, you can stand on this promise: the church is indestructible. Not because of us but because of Christ.

The imagery Jesus uses—"the gates of hell"—suggests that the church is not merely surviving but advancing. Gates are defensive structures, meaning the church is on offense, moving forward into the most broken places of the world, and even hell's defenses can't hold back the mission of God. Even when it seems like the gates of hell are prevailing over your life, your family, or your church, God will have the final say.

I know this not just theologically but experientially.

When we planted our church, we were portable for many years. As we now celebrate our twenty-year anniversary, I can honestly say that twelve of those years were incredibly tough. We set up and tore down our entire church for 624 Sundays—across eight different locations. And there were moments when it truly felt like the gates of hell were prevailing against us.

I'll never forget one season in particular. We were finally experiencing real momentum—people were coming to Christ, and the church was growing. But then, an older couple in our church, Martin and Mary, who saw themselves as the "spiritual parents" of the congregation, began to resist some of the unconventional ways we were doing ministry. One example? We allowed people to wear ball caps in our sanctuary, which at the time was a middle school gymnasium. They confronted me, demanding we change our approach to fit their preferences. I refused, explaining, "We're reaching people who don't usually go to church. This church doesn't exist to serve the preferences of those already here; we exist for those who have yet to come."

That didn't sit well. Their disapproval spiraled into a campaign of criticism and false accusations. They contacted our denominational leaders to have me removed. Though our leaders investigated and found no wrongdoing—only differences in vision—the damage was done. The couple lingered, sowing division and even standing outside the school where we met (at a literal gate like Absalom), trying to pull people away. Eventually, our network leadership stepped in and asked them to leave.

But their campaign didn't end there. They began calling every donor in our church, trying to convince them to stop giving. The impact was devastating. We lost 35 percent of our revenue and nearly 40 percent of our attendance. I was crushed. The financial strain became so severe that I had to take a significant pay cut, and as a result, we lost the first home we had ever purchased in California.

It felt like everything we had built was unraveling.

But even then, God was not finished. What looked like a setback was the setup for a comeback. He was still building His church, even when I couldn't see it.

But I didn't give up because of God's grace and the mentors He placed in my life who encouraged me when I wanted to quit.

And looking back now, I can say that the gates of hell didn't prevail.

About a year after that crisis, we experienced a fresh wave of growth. In fact, we were able to send out a group from our church to plant a new congregation on the other side of town, and that church is thriving today. So are we.

God is the builder of His church. And He is also the one who guards it against every dark force that tries to tear it down.

Maybe you're in a dark season right now. Maybe it feels like the gates of hell are winning. Please don't lose hope. God can bring you through. If you stay faithful, He will write a resurrection story you never saw coming.

You are part of something that cannot be defeated. That's why your church matters.

THE CHURCH WAS ALWAYS MEANT TO BE THE CENTER

The idea of running to the brokenness before planting a church isn't a new one—in fact, it's rooted deeply in church history. In colonial America, churches were deliberately placed at the geographical center of towns, serving as the nucleus for both spiritual and civic life. These meetinghouses were often the largest buildings in the community and functioned as spaces for worship, decision-making, and public gatherings.

One of the most vivid examples of this design is found in Annapolis, Maryland. In 1694, city planner Sir Francis Nicholson designed Annapolis with a Baroque street layout that placed St. Anne's Church at the center of what's now called Church Circle. The church is encircled by roads, with streets radiating outward like spokes on a wheel, literally placing the church at the heart of the city's life.

When my family and I visited Annapolis about ten years ago, I saw this powerful image firsthand. That city design gave me a visual of what the church used to be—and what it could be again. The church used to be the hub of the community, touching every part of life. And in a broken world like ours, I believe it's more important than ever that we reclaim that vision.

Long before the term "social enterprise" or "compassion ministry" existed, Catholic missionaries demonstrated the power of meeting real needs before expecting spiritual transformation.

When Catholic missions entered unreached or underserved areas—whether in Africa, Latin America, or Asia—they almost never started by constructing a cathedral. Instead, they began by identifying and addressing the most urgent needs in the community. In many places, this meant building hospitals to care for the sick or schools to educate children who would otherwise be left behind. These services weren't just strategies; they were spiritual acts of compassion. They embodied the gospel before preaching it.

They didn't just bring doctrine. They brought dignity.

In time, as trust grew and lives were impacted, these communities became fertile soil for faith. The churches that eventually formed were deeply rooted in the goodwill and tangible love already shown by these early missionaries. They didn't demand spiritual conversion before offering help—they served first and then invited people into the kingdom.

Long before many churches thought about starting with food pantries, schools, or job training, early missionaries were already running toward the most urgent needs of their communities, like physical suffering and the absence of basic healthcare. They went where pain was greatest, where systems had failed, and where no one else wanted to go. In doing so, they built trust, gained access, planted seeds of faith that would blossom into churches and movements, and transformed cultures.

This strategy—hospitals before sanctuaries, healing before preaching—is not only historical; it's profoundly biblical and still deeply effective today. Some of the most effective missionary movements in history followed this exact model.

HISTORICAL EXAMPLES BY REGION AND ERA

China: late nineteenth to early twentieth century

How they ran to the brokenness: Missionaries like Hudson Taylor and Dr. Peter Parker saw the brokenness of a culture ravaged by disease and distrust. In a nation deeply suspicious of foreign influence, they didn't start by planting churches—they opened clinics. These were often the first (and only) places where the sick and poor could receive care.

Impact:
- Medical ministry softened cultural hostility and opened once-closed cities to missionary presence.
- Hospitals became trusted institutions that introduced thousands to the love of Christ through compassionate care.
- Church planting naturally followed as relationships formed through years of medical service.

India: early twentieth century

How they ran to the brokenness: Dr. Ida Scudder, shocked by the deaths of women denied care due to cultural taboos, dedicated her life to filling that specific gap. She founded Christian Medical College (CMC) in Vellore, a place where female patients were treated with dignity and skill.

Impact:
- CMC became a gospel witness to thousands of students, doctors, and patients.
- Many Indian believers today trace their spiritual lineage to the witness they encountered in this place of healing.

- The college has trained generations of Indian medical professionals who now combine medical expertise with faith-driven compassion.

Africa: late nineteenth century to today

How they ran to the brokenness: In rural Africa, physical access to healthcare was nonexistent. Presbyterian and Baptist missionaries, as well as those from organizations like SIM, saw medical work not as a side project but as the tip of the spear. They journeyed into disease-stricken, underserved villages and stayed, often at great personal cost.

Impact:
- These hospitals became centers of hope long before any church was established.
- As people experienced physical healing, they opened up to spiritual transformation.
- Indigenous leaders were trained to continue both the medical and ministry work, resulting in sustainable local churches.

Middle East and North Africa: present day

How they run to the brokenness now: In restrictive nations where churches cannot be built and public evangelism is illegal, medical professionals are often the only legal "missionaries." Doctors and nurses work quietly and faithfully in hospitals or clinics, often sponsored by nongovernmental organizations (NGOs).

Impact:
- Healing opens doors that preaching alone cannot.
- Conversations happen around hospital beds, not pulpits.

› These relationships often evolve into underground house churches or informal discipleship communities—a modern-day version of Acts-style ministry.

This "healing first" model continues to flourish in the most unreached, devastated, and gospel-resistant parts of the world. Why? Because it mirrors Jesus's own ministry: "He sent them to preach the kingdom of God, and to heal the sick" (Luke 9:2, KJV).

Where this strategy works today:
› Creative access nations (e.g., Afghanistan, North Korea)
› Post-crisis zones (e.g., earthquake, famine, refugee camps)
› Tribal regions where no gospel infrastructure exists

HUB AUDIT: *How central is your church to the life of your community?*

If your church disappeared tomorrow, would your community notice?

Here are five reflective questions to help you evaluate whether your church is functioning as a true hub—spiritually, socially, and economically:

1) How visible are we in our community? Even if your physical location isn't in a prominent area, you can still be a visible and influential presence.
   » Are you regularly mentioned in community conversations?
   » Are you represented at local events or city meetings?
   » Do people know what you stand for and how to find you when they need help?

Practical Step: Consider what you're known for beyond Sunday services. What would your community say about you?

2) Is our reputation solid? Reputation is currency; it either opens doors or closes them.
   » Are you known as a generous, trustworthy, and consistent church?
   » Do people speak well of you—even those who don't attend?
   » Are you known for what you're for rather than just what you're against?

   Proverbs 22:1 says, "A good name is more desirable than great riches; to be esteemed is better than silver or gold."

3) Do people in the community trust us? Trust isn't automatic; it's earned.
   » When a crisis hits, do people instinctively turn to your church?
   » Are civic leaders, schools, nonprofits, or businesses willing to partner with you?
   » Do your neighbors believe you care about them, not just about growing your church?

   Trust is the bridge that allows spiritual transformation to come into people's lives. Without it, access is cut off.

4) Do other organizations come to us in times of crisis? One of the clearest indicators of being a hub is that people come to you when it matters most. In 2022, a tragic shooting rocked a local high school in our city. The school district was reeling. Tensions were high, emotions even higher. To my surprise, the superintendent

of the public school district—in California, a state not exactly known for being church-friendly—called and asked if they could use our sanctuary for a community meeting. The mayor came. Elected officials came. School board members and nonprofit leaders came. And then something happened that I'll never forget. They asked me—a local pastor—to open the meeting with a prayer of healing.

That moment said everything.

They didn't just need a venue. They needed a voice of hope. And they knew where to find it.

5) Are we meeting the felt needs of our community? Spiritual transformation is our highest aim, but felt needs open the door.
   » Are you helping people with food, housing, clothing, jobs, or mental health?
   » Do people see your church as a place of tangible help, not just religious services?
   » Are you listening to the pain in your city?

Matthew 25:35 reminds us: "I was hungry and you gave me something to eat, I was thirsty and you gave me something to drink."

How'd you do?

If you answered "no" or "not sure" to more than one of these questions, you may be more peripheral than central to your community. That's not a failure—it's a call to action. You *can* become the hub. But it starts with honest reflection and a willingness to run to the brokenness.

ENVISIONING YOUR CHURCH AS THE HUB

You may have heard teaching on vision so often that it feels overdone—but I'll be honest: if *you*, as a leader, don't see your church as the hub of your community, no one else will. We must lead with one foot planted in today's reality and the other stepping toward God's preferred future.

Imagine your church becoming the place where believers from diverse backgrounds come together, united in love and mission, seeking to glorify God. The local church is the only organization in your community where people voluntarily gather for one eternal purpose. That alone sets it apart—and gives it unmatched potential.

You are uniquely positioned. And you are called not just to host people but to heal communities. To not just gather people but to send them. When you start to see your church this way—as a living, breathing hub of hope—you lead others to see it too.

FROM PERSECUTED PASTOR TO LOCAL HERO

There are places in the world where the name of Jesus is not just unwelcome; it's dangerous—tribal regions with no gospel infrastructure, where following Christ comes at great personal cost. One of those places is Sri Lanka.

I was there recently, walking through a remote village surrounded by breathtaking beauty—the kind of place that makes you forget, for a moment, the harsh spiritual resistance that lingers just below the surface. The air was thick with the scent of the jungle, and the sun beat down hard. And yet, there was joy in the eyes of the man I came to visit.

His name was Amarasiri, a local pastor quietly leading a small house church in the heart of a region dominated by Buddhism and Hinduism. Just two years ago, Amarasiri experienced the kind of persecution we only read about. The local villagers, angered by his refusal to stop preaching the name of Jesus, gave him an ultimatum: deny Christ or leave.

He chose neither. So, they burned his house to the ground.

Everything was gone. His home, his possessions, the little security his family had reduced to ashes because of the gospel.

But he stayed.

And now, just a short time later, I stood with him as our team delivered clean water filters and bags of food to his village, not just to his congregation but to the same public school that had once turned him away. In these remote places, water sources are polluted, and clean drinking water is scarce. And here was this man, once seen as a threat, now providing for the very people who had persecuted him.

He told me, with tears in his eyes, that everything changed when the community realized the church wasn't just preaching hope; it was bringing it.

The villagers who once treated him as a pariah now see him as a provider. The man whose home was destroyed now helps build up the lives of others. And the name of Jesus, once rejected, is now being whispered in homes and welcomed in hearts.

Pastor Amarasiri is no longer seen as a local villain. He is now viewed as a local hero.

This story isn't just about one man's courage. It's a living example of what can happen when we choose to run toward the brokenness even when it's risky, even when it's unrewarded, even when it costs everything. Because in the kingdom of God, seeds sown in ashes often grow into movements of hope.

 ## RUNNING TO BROKENNESS ISN'T ALWAYS PREACHING FIRST.

Let this challenge us: where are the places we're afraid to go? And who are the people we're called to love, even when it's not safe or easy?

Because the gospel always runs toward the broken. Even in Sri Lanka.

Organizations using this model:
- Samaritan's Purse: Sends field hospitals to disaster zones with a clear gospel presence.
- CMDA Global Health Outreach: Medical missions with evangelistic partnerships.
- Frontier Ventures: Uses long-term development projects to gain access.
- YWAM Medical Ships: Brings healthcare to remote areas like Papua New Guinea, along with discipleship.

Why does this still work? Because it shows the gospel; it doesn't just say it. It builds trust in places where Christianity is feared or misunderstood. It follows Jesus's model of compassionate presence. It plants roots for the long haul—healing both body and soul over time.

James warned: "Suppose a brother or sister is without clothes and daily food. If one of you says to them, 'Go in peace; keep warm and well fed,' but does nothing about their physical needs, what good is it?" (James 2:15-16) James's words remind us that faith is more than speech—it's action, and often, that action starts with meeting practical needs.

Running to brokenness isn't always preaching first. Sometimes, it's wrapping a bandage, administering an IV, or holding a mother's hand as she mourns. These actions speak a language deeper than doctrine—they reveal the heart of Christ. And that's often where the church is truly born.

This principle is deeply aligned with the model of Jesus Himself.

Jesus fed the hungry before He preached the Sermon on the Mount. He healed the blind man before inviting him into discipleship. He ministered to bodies, minds, and souls—because He understood that brokenness is not just spiritual; it's physical, emotional, and relational too.

In many ways, that's exactly what we're doing at LifeBridge and through our ACTS Foundation. (a non-profit that we began to meet the social needs of the community) We didn't start by asking our city to show up for Sunday service. We started by asking: "Where does it hurt? Where is the community most broken? And how can we, as the church, bring healing?"

We began with food insecurity, job training, addiction recovery, and housing support—and as we met those needs, we earned the right to be heard. Like the missionaries who came before us, we're building trust and transforming lives—not just spiritually but socially and economically too.

Churches that run to the brokenness will eventually become the most trusted voice in the neighborhood—but only if we're willing to go to the streets, the shelters, and the margins before expecting anyone to come to the sanctuary.

Let me be clear: we are not replacing the gospel. We're revealing it through action.

This is what the early church did. This is what Jesus did. And this is what you and your church can do too.

While you may not be at a place in which you can start a medical clinic (we would love to do this in the future), these are just ideas to spur you on to identify some of the biggest needs in your community and to begin to meet those needs.

NOT ALL BROKENNESS LOOKS THE SAME

Maybe your church isn't located near obvious or visible brokenness. You might not see tent cities, food lines, or boarded-up buildings. But that doesn't mean the brokenness isn't there. In fact, it might be even closer than you think—just hidden behind manicured lawns and freshly painted fences.

Behind closed doors, families are hurting. Addiction, alcoholism, anxiety, and deep relational strain often go unnoticed. The pain is private. The wounds are internal. But make no mistake—they're real. Just because a neighborhood looks healthy on the outside doesn't mean it's whole on the inside.

The truth is that every church, no matter its location, size, or demographic, has brokenness right around the corner.

And if your church can recognize and respond to those needs—even the hidden ones—it can become the hub of healing and hope in your community. That's exactly how God designed the church to function. It's how the early church lived—positioned at the center of the city, both geographically and relationally.

It's time to reclaim that role.

If you're serving in a community where the need isn't obvious, here are a few intentional ways to uncover what's really going on:

1) Build Relationships with Local Schools. School counselors and administrators often know which kids are struggling due to problems at home—substance abuse, neglect, divorce, or domestic violence.
2) Connect with Law Enforcement or First Responders. Police, firefighters, and EMTs see behind the closed doors. They know the neighborhoods where overdose calls or domestic disputes happen frequently—even in "nice" areas.

3) Partner with Mental Health Professionals. Local therapists, recovery centers, and clinics often serve clients from high-income families facing emotional or relational breakdowns.
4) Offer Confidential Surveys or Listening Sessions. Sometimes, the best way to understand your community is simply to ask. Host safe spaces for open dialogue. People are often more honest than we expect when they feel heard.
5) Start with Your Own Church. Don't assume everyone in your congregation is thriving. Private pain often sits quietly in your own pews. Pastoral care, support groups, and one-on-one conversations can uncover needs that have been buried for years.

Your church can become the center of your community, not because it's flashy or famous, but because it runs to the pain, even when it's hidden. When you do that, your church becomes what it was always meant to be: a beacon of light, a house of healing, and a trusted hub of hope.

BEWARE OF THE COMPARISON TRAP

Unfortunately, far too many pastors—especially those in smaller churches—feel like they're failing simply because they don't have large crowds or budgets. I know I have felt that way at times. Some are considering leaving ministry altogether. Many already have. Why? Because we've adopted a narrow definition of success that values visibility over impact.

IF WE DEFINE SUCCESS ONLY BY WHAT HAPPENS ON SUNDAY, WE'RE MISSING OUT ON SIX OTHER DAYS OF KINGDOM OPPORTUNITY.

The apostle Paul writes in 2 Corinthians 10:12, "We do not dare to classify or compare ourselves with some who commend themselves. When they measure themselves by themselves and compare themselves with themselves, they are not wise."

Yet this is exactly what happens in far too many pastors' hearts. We compare. We question. We get discouraged. I truly believe that comparison is one of the enemy's most strategic tools to weaken the church, not by attacking its doctrine but by discouraging its leaders.

Every profession has occupational hazards. For a lineman, it might be the risk of falling from a power pole. For those of us in ministry, one of the greatest hazards is discouragement, especially the kind that comes from comparing our ministry to others. And while that discouragement may not break bones, it absolutely takes a toll on our mental health, our emotional energy, and our spiritual strength.

In chapter 9, we'll go deeper into those occupational hazards and how to guard against them. But here's the big idea I want to leave with you:

RUN TO THE BROKENNESS

If we define success only by what happens on Sunday, we're missing out on six other days of kingdom opportunity.

Here are the real questions I want to ask you:

How well are we running to the brokenness around us?

How are we bringing healing, hope, and help to our neighborhoods, not just in our services but in our streets?

Let's reimagine the local church—not by its size but by its reach.

Not by its seating capacity but by its sending capacity.

Not by attendance alone but by transformation.

Because whether your church has 50, 500, 5,000, or 50,000, you are fulfilling the heart of Christ for your community if you're running to the brokenness.

As followers of Jesus, we are not limited to what we see with our physical eyes. We've been filled with the Holy Spirit, who gives us discernment, wisdom, and vision to perceive needs before they're fully visible. We don't have to wait until the pain is obvious or the crisis is on our doorstep to act. Just like Nehemiah saw the broken walls of Jerusalem before anyone else named the problem, we are called to walk in spiritual awareness—to be the kind of leaders who see with heaven's eyes.

Our churches were never meant to be reactive institutions. They were meant to be prophetic communities—discerning the spiritual, social, and economic needs of our cities and stepping in with courage, compassion, and creativity.

And maybe you're like me—maybe you've felt unqualified when it comes to creativity. I've had moments where I doubted whether I had the ideas, the innovation, or the vision to respond to the need around me. But here's what I've learned: creativity isn't just a personality trait; it's a byproduct of the Holy Spirit living inside of you. The same Spirit who hovered over the waters in Genesis, who empowered the prophets and apostles, now dwells in you. Because of that, you are more creative than you think. You are anointed to solve problems, to build what doesn't exist yet, and to dream what others can't see.

So, let's ask God to open our eyes. Let's not wait for pain to go viral or problems to become public. Let's run to the brokenness before it makes the news. Because when the church leads with Spirit-filled vision and creativity, we become the kind of hub our communities can trust—one that doesn't just respond to brokenness but anticipates it . . . and brings the healing power of Jesus right into the middle of it.

APPLICATION

What's Your Brokenness?

Before you can lead your church to run to the brokenness, you must first recognize your own.

Take a moment to reflect:

- What areas of brokenness in your life has God redeemed?
- Where have you experienced pain, loss, injustice, or deep need?
- How might those experiences shape the way you lead and serve today?

Often, the places where we've been broken become the very places where God calls us to minister.

This week:
- Write out your own story of brokenness and redemption. Ask God to show you how it connects to your calling.
- Look at your church with fresh eyes. Where is your church already positioned near brokenness—but not yet engaged?
- Reach out to one person, organization, or school leader in your community and simply ask: "How can we serve you right now?"

Let this be your prayer:

"Lord, give me eyes to see the brokenness around me— and the courage to run toward it, not away from it."

Because if you'll start there, God will take you further than you ever imagined.

REFLECTION

1) What metrics have you been using to define success in your church? Are these metrics mostly numerical (e.g., attendance, budget)? How might you begin measuring spiritual, social, and economic impact more effectively?
2) If your church closed its doors tomorrow, would your community feel the impact? Why or why not? What are you currently known for in your neighborhood? How can you become more visible and valuable to your city?
3) In what ways might you be unintentionally comparing your church to others? How has comparison shaped your self-worth or your sense of calling? What truths from Scripture can help reframe your perspective?

4) What needs—spiritual, social, or economic—are going unmet in your community right now? What conversations, partnerships, or observations could help you identify hidden brokenness? How can your church begin to meet those needs in tangible ways?
5) Do you truly believe that Jesus is building His church, even when you can't see the growth? How does this belief (or lack of it) shape the way you lead? What would it look like to rest more deeply in God's sovereignty over your ministry?

CHAPTER 2

CHANGE THE METRICS

We're in a leadership crisis—and it's costing the church. Recent stats reveal just how serious it is:
- 80% of pastors believe ministry has negatively affected their families
- 75% report significant stress-related crises at least once in their ministry
- 72% work between 55–75 hours a week
- 52% feel overworked and unable to meet expectations
- 23% admit they feel distant from their families[4]

It's not just about stress. Nearly 40 percent of pastors today are seriously considering quitting ministry altogether.[5] But the leadership crisis we're facing goes beyond those currently serving—it's also about the next generation. Fewer and fewer young leaders are pursuing full-time ministry. Yes, financial limitations play a role, but there's a deeper issue beneath the

---
4 "Statistics in Ministry," *Pastoral Care,* updated 2025, https://www.pastoralcareinc.com/statistics/.
5 Barna, "Pastors Share Top Reasons They've Considered Quitting Ministry in the Past Year."

surface. I believe we need to redefine what success in ministry really means.

 **SUCCESS IN THE KINGDOM ISN'T ABOUT HOW MANY PEOPLE SIT IN YOUR SEATS—IT'S ABOUT HOW MANY LIVES YOU IMPACT.**

For too long, we've measured ministry success by attendance, buildings, and budgets. But those metrics alone are no longer inspiring to many emerging leaders. In fact, some of the most passionate, mission-minded young leaders I've met are not rejecting *ministry*—they're rejecting the narrow definitions of ministry success they've seen modeled. And who can blame them? If we continue to hold up platform size as the primary marker of effectiveness, we'll keep losing creative, courageous, and even *called* leaders who want something more meaningful—something that looks like the ministry of Jesus, who ran to the margins, lifted the broken, and flipped the script on status.

In Chapter 8: "Funding the Mission," I'll offer creative solutions to help alleviate some of the practical reservations younger leaders have about entering ministry—including how churches can build sustainable models that provide both impact and income. In this chapter, I want to make the case that we need to change the metrics. If we want to raise up the next generation of leaders, we need to stop asking, *How many are sitting in the seats?* and start asking, *How many lives are being impacted beyond the walls?*

Why?

Because for decades, we've been trained to believe that success equals Sunday attendance, tithes, and offerings. We've been measured by how full the sanctuary is, how many seats are filled, and how much money came in the offering plate. And let's be honest—it's crushing many of us.

I've felt it myself. On Sundays when the sanctuary was full, I felt invincible. But when we were down by sixty people? I felt like a failure. Here's the truth God has taught me over time: success in the kingdom isn't about how many people sit in your seats—it's about how many lives you impact.

THE WAKE-UP CALL: COVID-19

The pandemic was brutal—but it forced a much-needed shift in how we define success. COVID-19 has often been called "the great disruptor," and for us, it certainly lived up to that name.

At LifeBridge, we had to face hard questions:

Who are we really serving?

How are we helping people beyond Sunday?

Are we only focused on spiritual needs, or are we addressing social and economic needs too?

There was a significant shift from how we did ministry before the pandemic. In many ways, what began as a response to crisis ended up becoming a completely new model for ministry—one that has reshaped the heart and focus of our church.

Before, our efforts were primarily centered on spiritual impact, and that will always remain our foundation. But we began to sense that God was calling us to go deeper. Instead of only preparing people for heaven, we felt compelled to bring a piece of heaven to people's lives here on earth.

We started asking new questions:

What if the church could help people put food on the table?

What if we could help families stay housed and employed?

What if the church became the center of healing, provision, and transformation in our community?

That shift in mindset changed everything for us. We began to see church not just as a place for worship but as a launchpad for hope, where people could find both spiritual renewal and practical support. It redefined what we believed the church could and should be.

Today, we're impacting around 6,000 people a month, not because they all sit in our services but because we run to the brokenness through:

- Grocery giveaways
- Senior citizen delivery programs
- Patrons in our event center
- Families in our preschool
- People connected through our church family

For years, our thrift store was part of this reach, employing and supporting people in need. Even after we paused that ministry at the end of last year, our impact has only grown. People who had never attended our church began saying,

"LifeBridge is that church that really helps people." Some assumed we were a megachurch because of our outreach footprint. We are not a megachurch in size, but we have a mega impact, and I believe every church, no matter its size, can redefine its metrics for success and multiply its reach.

What could this look like for your church?

- Food ministry: grocery giveaways, food pantries, or partnerships with local agencies
- Clothing drives: regular distribution to families in need
- Housing support: helping people secure stable housing
- Job creation: hiring underemployed or hard-to-employ people within your ministries or businesses
- Community services: preschools, event centers, counseling, after-school programs

FROM PRESCHOOL PERFORMANCE TO A LIFE TRANSFORMED

Michael and Lacey hadn't regularly attended church since their teenage years. Like so many young families, life had gotten busy, and work, kids, routines, and faith had taken a backseat. God was still in their hearts, but He wasn't a part of their daily rhythms. Church just wasn't on the radar.

That all changed one Sunday morning.

They came to our church not for a sermon, worship, or even out of spiritual curiosity. They came to watch their daughter perform in a preschool program hosted in our sanctuary. It was a sweet, simple event, just kids being kids. But something unexpected happened. As they sat in that room, surrounded by the love and warmth of our church community, something stirred in their hearts. They didn't just see a church. They felt like they had come home.

That Sunday, they came for their daughter's preschool program. But they've been attending every Sunday since.

If we had never launched our preschool as a social enterprise, designed to meet a practical need in our city, Michael and Lacey may have never walked through the doors. And if they hadn't walked through the doors, they may have missed the life change that was waiting for them.

Since then, both have rededicated their lives to Jesus. Lacey now serves on our children's ministry team, pouring into children the way others once poured into hers. And Michael co-leads our men's ministry, "Man Cave," helping other men grow in their faith and walk in community.

This is what it means to change the metrics.

They weren't reached through a billboard, a church campaign, or a revival service (all worthy ways to reach people). They were reached through a preschool. Through a need in their family that intersected with a need our church had chosen to meet.

When you measure success only by Sunday attendance or offering totals, you miss the full picture of how God is working. But when you shift your mindset, when you start seeing your preschool, your food bank, your event center, or your job-training program as ministry, everything changes.

Michael and Lacey are proof: when your church steps into the needs of your community, you don't just serve the city, you help restore souls.

THE PROBLEM WITH OLD METRICS

Measuring the right things matters. If we want to lead churches that truly reflect the heart of Jesus, we need to reevaluate how we define success.

Traditional church metrics have included:
- Sunday attendance
- Tithes and offerings
- Salvations and baptisms
- Small group participation
- Volunteer engagement

These metrics are important, but they're incomplete. And they can be spiritually dangerous if we elevate them as the only measure of success.

JUDGING SUCCESS ONLY BY NUMBERS IS A DOUBLE-EDGED SWORD.

As leaders, we need to recognize how fragile these numbers are. A drop in attendance or giving can shake our confidence, discourage our team, and leave us questioning our calling. I've been there; you probably have too.

Judging success only by numbers is a double-edged sword. When things are up, you feel great. When things are down, you feel like you're failing. But here's the deeper issue: when we rely solely on traditional church metrics—attendance, giving, and group participation—we unintentionally train our congregations to do the same. They begin to evaluate your leadership only through that narrow lens. And if those numbers aren't strong, you may find yourself unfairly judged—not because you're ineffective, but because the metrics are incomplete. That's why it's so important to expand how we measure ministry impact. But what if God wants us to measure impact in a much broader way?

A BIBLICAL SHIFT

In Matthew 25, Jesus tells the parable of the sheep and the goats. And notice what He celebrates:

"For I was hungry and you gave me something to eat,
I was thirsty and you gave me something to drink,
I was a stranger and you invited me in,
I needed clothes and you clothed me,
I was sick and you looked after me,
I was in prison and you came to visit me."
—Matthew 25:35-36

Jesus doesn't say, "Well done—you packed out your Sunday services." He says, "Well done—you served the least of these."

What if we began to measure church success based on the metrics Jesus laid out here in Matthew?

- How many people has your church fed?
- How many people has your church clothed?
- How many sick people have you comforted or guided back to health?
- How many prisoners is your church actively reaching?

- How many widows have you helped?
- How many orphans have you assisted?

Once again, most Western churches measure success by attendance, giving, and group participation. And while those are not bad metrics, they fall far short of the kingdom standard. Jesus redefines success around compassion, action, and proximity to the broken. If we want to hear "Well done," maybe we need to start counting differently.

 **WHEN YOU ARE OBEDIENT, GOD BRINGS THE GROWTH.**

The early church understood this. Acts 2:44 and 47 say: "All the believers were together and had everything in common. They sold property and possessions to give to anyone who had need.... And the Lord added to their number daily those who were being saved."

What was the result of this kind of sacrificial, holistic love? God brought the growth.

When a church sets its heart on meeting the needs of the broken, God blesses it—sometimes in ways we never expect. But that kind of growth doesn't always happen overnight. And it shouldn't be the motive.

We don't serve the broken to spark the latest church growth trend. We serve the broken because it's what Jesus told us to do.

Growth is not the goal; obedience is. But here's the beautiful truth: when you are obedient, God brings the growth.

Today, our church is 25 percent larger than we were before COVID-19. I give all the credit to God and to a simple, consistent commitment to doing what Jesus described in Matthew 25. The more we focused on running to the brokenness and the less we obsessed over Sunday metrics, the more people began showing up on Sunday mornings.

Obedience first. Growth second. That's the kingdom way.

A STORY THAT CHANGED ME

One of the most powerful reminders of why we do what we do came through a young man named Jonathan—a young adult with special needs.

We first met Jonathan through a community program that partners with nonprofits by providing labor support in exchange for job training and experience. Since our thrift store requires a lot of hands-on work—sorting clothes, organizing inventory, and managing donations—it was a great fit for both sides.

Jonathan quickly became a valued part of the team. When the program ended, the organization asked if we'd consider hiring him permanently. We didn't hesitate. Despite his disability, we saw his worth, not just in what he could do but in who he was. We believed he had something unique to bring, and more importantly, we believed in giving him a real chance.

We hired him the following week.

CHANGE THE METRICS

One afternoon, not long after he started, something happened I'll never forget. It was payday. Our thrift store manager handed Jonathan his first paycheck—the first one he had ever received in his entire life. He opened the envelope, stared at it for a moment, and then began to weep. Through tears, he said, "I've never earned money before. This is my first real job."

In that moment, we didn't just pay someone for hours worked. We restored dignity. We gave Jonathan something more than a paycheck—we gave him a sense of purpose, a place to belong, and the joy of meaningful contribution.

Still holding his check, Jonathan immediately asked to call his mom. When she answered, he could barely speak through his tears. "Mom, I got my first paycheck ever!" She cried with him. So did we.

But there's more to the story.

What made the difference wasn't just the job—it was our team. They *loved on Jonathan*, encouraged him, and welcomed him without hesitation. They didn't just show up for work—they showed up as the church. They lived out the culture of grace, compassion, and community that made Christianity attractive to him. Jonathan saw the gospel not just preached but *lived* through kindness, patience, and belonging.

That should count in the metrics.

Stories like this remind me that real success is far beyond Sunday morning attendance. It looks like lives changed in unexpected places—like a thrift store aisle, a first paycheck, or a restored sense of purpose. It's about building ministries that do more than gather crowds—they give people a future.

Since that day, Jonathan has become a regular part of our church family. A few months after joining us on Sundays, he gave his life to Jesus. Today, he faithfully serves on our tech team, not because we preached a great message but because we created a culture that reflected Christ.

Here's the truth: Jonathan may have never walked into our church if we hadn't started that thrift store. He may have never earned that first paycheck or encountered the love of Jesus in such a tangible way. That's why we must rethink our ministry models and our metrics. When churches step into creative spaces like social enterprise, we do more than raise money—we raise people. We give them hope, purpose, dignity, and the chance to experience the beauty of the gospel through everyday work and everyday love.

On the Sundays when attendance is down and discouragement knocks at my door, God reminds me of people like Jonathan—and that keeps me going.

NEW METRICS TO CONSIDER

Too often, the only numbers churches measure are Sunday attendance, offering totals, and maybe small group participation. While those metrics are helpful, they fall far short of the holistic impact the church is called to make. If we are serious about becoming hubs of transformation, we must expand our scoreboard.

Here are some new metrics to consider when running to the brokenness:

1) **Spiritual Impact**

Are people encountering Jesus? It's important to clarify: we're not promoting what some might call a *social gospel*. Running to the brokenness doesn't mean we forget the main mission; it means we live it out more fully. We exist to see people enter a thriving relationship with God and to take as many people to heaven with us as we can.

Are they growing in discipleship? Are they learning, growing, and being shaped by Scripture and community over time?

Are they serving and using their gifts? When people come alive in Christ, they begin to serve others. Are you creating space for that to happen?

2) **Social Impact**

How many people are you feeding? Since the pandemic, we've had the honor of distributing (as of this writing) 1.6 million pounds of food. We live in what's considered the third most food-insecure region in the US. This is an obvious area of brokenness in our backyard and an obvious area where the church must respond.

How many are you clothing, helping to find housing, or walking with through crisis? Before we paused our thrift store ministry, we were clothing approximately 1,500 people per month. Each one of those individuals mattered deeply to God.

One afternoon, I was standing just outside our thrift store, looking at a rack labeled: *Grab a bag full of clothes for just $1*. A young woman approached and asked if she was limited to just one bag. When I asked why, she explained that she worked at a local charter school and had twenty graduating seniors who couldn't afford decent clothes—many of whom had job interviews coming up. I invited her to bring them all on a special shopping trip to our store, free of charge.

A few weeks later, twenty high school seniors walked in—most for the first time in a store where they could choose their own clothing. Watching them pick outfits, laugh, ask for advice, and hold their heads a little higher was one of the most fulfilling moments of ministry I've ever experienced. That day, we didn't just give away clothes. We gave away dignity. We gave away confidence. We gave away hope.

That should count for something on a stat sheet somewhere.

How are you helping the most vulnerable in your city? Every community has hidden needs. Maybe it's children in foster care, seniors who can't drive, or refugee families just trying to find their footing. If you're not sure where to begin, ask God to open a door for you. You never know how that open door will provide a path for you to impact your community in a creative way!

3) **Economic Impact**

Are you helping the unemployed or underemployed? At one of our recent staff meetings, something unforgettable happened. Amanda, a young woman we had recently hired as the event manager for our Buena Vista Event Center, stood to share a testimony. Her voice trembled slightly as she spoke—not from nervousness but from the weight of what she was about to say. She began, "I wouldn't know Jesus if it weren't for this event center." She went on to explain that she and her husband, Adam, had gotten married at our venue. But then, with tears in her eyes and courage in her voice, she admitted something deeply personal: "Neither of us really remembers much from that day—because we were both so drunk. I'm ashamed to say that. But what I do remember is how your staff cared for us. They didn't judge us. They just loved us."

That simple act of kindness left an imprint. Not long after the wedding, Amanda and Adam decided to visit our church. Something clicked. They kept coming. They gave their lives to Jesus. And everything started to change. As one of our pastors walked with them in discipleship, Amanda eventually shared that they were struggling financially, barely making ends meet. Around that time, a position opened at the event center. We hired her.

Now, standing before our staff, Amanda shared the full picture: "This church—this place—didn't just change my life spiritually. It changed it economically. I look forward to my Buena Vista direct deposit because it means I can make my rent." You could feel the room shift as she spoke. There wasn't a dry eye in the room. Her story is proof that when a church runs to the brokenness—when we step into the spiritual, social, and economic needs of people—heaven takes notice and lives are transformed. Amanda's journey should be counted as a worthy metric because this is what the kingdom looks like: one act of kindness, one job offer, one open door at a time. Amanda is only one example—we've seen God use our social enterprises to employ people coming out of incarceration, adults with disabilities, and single parents who just needed a chance.

Are you helping people gain skills to provide for their families? Whether it's job training, resume prep, or helping someone get certified in a trade, you open the door to spiritual transformation when you help people thrive economically.

By embracing these expanded metrics—spiritual, social, and economic—you'll begin to see your church not just as a place people attend but as a force for transformation in your city.

SCRIPTURE TO ANCHOR THIS SHIFT

James 2:14-17 reminds us:

> *What good is it, my brothers and sisters, if someone claims to have faith but has no deeds? Can such faith save them? Suppose a brother or a sister is without clothes and daily food. If one of you says to them, "Go in peace; keep warm and well fed," but does nothing about their physical needs, what good is it? In the same way, faith by itself, if it is not accompanied by action, is dead.*

It was a significant shift from how we did ministry before the pandemic. In many ways, what began as a crisis response evolved into a completely new model—one that's now central to who we are.

We used to focus almost exclusively on spiritual impact—and that will always be our foundation. But during those disruptive years, we began to sense the Lord asking us to go further. We didn't just want to prepare people for heaven; we wanted to bring glimpses of heaven into people's lives *right now*. That meant giving people the ability to provide for their families, put food on the table, and keep a roof over their heads.

We started asking bold questions:
What if the church could help someone find a job?
What if we could stop the cycle of homelessness?
What if the church became the most trusted place in a city, not just for prayer but for provision, employment, restoration, and belonging?

That shift in mindset changed everything. Our view of what the church *could* be—and *should* be—was completely transformed.

And if you want to know what this looks like in real life, let me tell you about Maria.

Maria came to Fresno from the Midwest—but not by choice. She had recently been released from prison, and because of the nature of her crimes, one of the conditions of her release was that she had to remain in this region for the next ten years. She had no family here. No support system. And most tragically, because of the severity and stigma of what she had done, no one wanted to give her a second chance.

She was unhireable. Untouchable. Unwanted.

But Maria showed up at our thrift store and asked to volunteer. She was in her late thirties and had nothing to offer but her time and willingness. She kept coming back—week after week—for over a year. And when she demonstrated consistency and faithfulness, we hired her.

What happened next had nothing to do with a sermon or a stage. It had everything to do with the culture of our team. The love of Jesus was so tangible in that store—so present in the way our people worked and welcomed—that Maria slowly opened her heart again.

RUN TO THE BROKENNESS

She started coming to LifeBridge.
She reconnected with the faith she once knew as a child.
And before long, Maria gave her life fully to Jesus.
Now, she's not just employed. She's not just restored.
She's redeemed.

Let me be clear: had our thrift store not been there—had that opportunity not existed—Maria may never have found her way back. She may have become another lost story in a broken system. Instead, Maria is a living, breathing *metric* of what happens when the church steps into the mess with both compassion and courage.

Her story is evidence of the real power of the gospel at work—not just in the sanctuary but in everyday spaces.

 **WE DON'T RUN TO THE BROKENNESS JUST TO FILL SEATS ON SUNDAY.**

And perhaps most remarkably, because of this opportunity, the odds of Maria becoming a repeat offender—of going back to the life she came from—have dropped dramatically.

That's not just spiritual impact.
That's social transformation.
That's kingdom work.
And that absolutely should count as a major metric.

CHANGE THE METRICS

This is why we must change the metrics.

Because in God's economy, every soul matters. Every story matters.

And when one woman from the Midwest—unhireable, unwanted, and forgotten—finds dignity, purpose, and salvation, that's the kind of success heaven celebrates.

Isaiah 58:10 gives us a powerful promise: "If you spend yourselves in behalf of the hungry and satisfy the needs of the oppressed, then your light will rise in the darkness, and your night will become like the noonday."

We've seen this promise come to life in our church.

God has blessed us in countless ways—ways that don't always show up on the traditional scorecard. Sure, all three of our services are now packed, and we're actively looking for a larger sanctuary (which, admittedly, is a good problem to have). But I need to be clear: we don't run to the brokenness just to fill seats on Sunday.

Yes, I want people in church on Sundays. I want lives transformed by the Word, worship, and community. But that's not *why* we serve. That's not *why* we go into the streets, open food pantries, build job programs, or start social enterprises.

We do it because God commanded us to.

Isaiah doesn't say, "If you build a bigger church, your light will rise." He says, *"If you spend yourselves on behalf of the hungry . . . then your light will rise in the darkness."* That's the metric God cares about. That's the kind of ministry He blesses.

We've seen that blessing, not just in attendance but in impact, not just in budgets but in lives changed.

So, if your church is running to the brokenness and not seeing the traditional results right away, *keep going.* Heaven is tracking things differently. Your faithfulness, your compassion, your obedience—those are the real metrics that matter.

Let's stop measuring only what happens inside the walls of the sanctuary. Let's start measuring how much light is breaking through the darkness because we chose to spend ourselves on behalf of others.

That's the kind of church I want to build. That's the kind of leader I want to be.

METRICS TRACKING TOOLS FOR CHURCHES

You don't need expensive software to start tracking meaningful impact, but here are some helpful options:

- Google Sheets or Excel → simple tracking of numbers + stories
- Planning Center → track groups, volunteers, and attendance
- Church Community Builder (CCB) → track giving, engagement, and outreach
- Elvanto, Breeze, or Rock RMS → good all-in-one church management tools
- Custom Dashboard → assign someone on your team to track outreach + social impact numbers monthly

Most importantly: track stories, not just statistics. Make sure you're recording the lives changed, not just the boxes checked.

IT'S TIME TO EXPAND THE SCORECARD

You might be asking, *"Are you just moving the goalposts so churches can feel better about mediocre Sundays?"*

No—absolutely not.

What I'm suggesting is that for decades, the church has had its goalposts set too narrowly. It's time to redefine the goalposts—not lower them.

The local church is perfectly positioned to meet the spiritual, social, and economic needs of its community, frankly, better than any other organization or faith-based nonprofit. And when we start measuring that impact, we won't just survive—we'll thrive. And just like in Acts 2, the Lord will add to our number daily.

APPLICATION

- Gather your leadership team. Ask: "What are we measuring now? What's missing from our scorecard?"
- Define one new metric for each category (spiritual, social, economic). Example: spiritual → number of people in discipleship; social → families fed monthly; economic → people placed in jobs.
- Start small. Don't overhaul everything at once. Pilot one project—like a job skills workshop or new food distribution program.
- Communicate wins. Share stories like Jonathan's regularly with your church. Celebrate Monday–Saturday impact from the pulpit.
- Pray over your metrics. Ask God to help you see beyond numbers to the real lives behind each one.

REFLECTION

1) Which traditional metrics have defined success in your ministry?
2) How has that shaped your sense of identity or worth as a leader?
3) Where is your church already making social or economic impact, even if you've never measured it?
4) What new metrics could you begin tracking this month?
5) How could shifting your metrics change the culture of your leadership team?
6) What's one new ministry or service your church could offer to meet community needs?

CHAPTER 3

IDENTIFY THE NEED

If all you're doing is having church on Sunday, it will be difficult—if not impossible—to become a true community hub.

Pastor David loved his church. Nestled in a quiet neighborhood, it had a solid core of faithful attendees, a worship team that could hold its own, and a kids' ministry that ran smoothly every Sunday. From the outside, everything looked . . . fine. But "fine" wasn't transforming the neighborhood.

Just a few blocks away, brokenness pulsed under the surface. A single mom struggled to choose between groceries and rent. A teenager wrestled with anxiety and had nowhere safe to turn. An elderly veteran sat alone in his apartment, hoping someone might check in. And yet, the church remained unaware—content, busy, but blind.

It wasn't that Pastor David didn't care. It's that no one had ever taught him to ask the right questions. Sunday was full, so Monday through Saturday stayed empty. The doors were open but only for services.

And then one day, after a midweek prayer meeting, a neighbor showed up at the church office—not for spiritual advice but to ask if someone could help them find a warm meal. Pastor David froze. He had no idea what to offer. That encounter haunted him. It wasn't just the church that had missed the need—it was him. The brokenness had been there all along.

If all you're doing is having church on Sunday, it will be difficult—if not impossible—to become a true community hub.

 **DON'T NORMALIZE BROKENNESS; RUN TO THE BROKENNESS, AND DO SOMETHING ABOUT IT.**

I've learned this firsthand: when you ask God to help you meet the needs of your community, and you truly mean it, God will open doors you never dreamed possible.

Sometimes, the need stares you right in the face.

When my wife and I first moved to Fresno, we kept noticing shopping carts everywhere. It was an eyesore, but more than that, it symbolized brokenness. I brought it up to our tiny launch group, and at first, they hadn't even noticed—it had become normal to them. That's the funny thing about brokenness, whether it be in our own personal lives, the church, or the community. We become accustomed to the brokenness, which is one of the greatest barriers to running to the brokenness. Don't normalize the brokenness; do something about it.

So, on a sunny Saturday morning, four of us loaded up pickup trucks and spent the day collecting stray shopping carts and returning them to stores. The managers were thrilled. But not everyone was: two men in a box truck angrily told us we were cutting into their business. (They were paid per cart.)

Even though we unintentionally cost them money, that day marked the DNA of our church—a church that would not become numb to the brokenness in its city.

THE CHURCH EXISTS FOR THOSE WHO AREN'T HERE YET

Many churches fall into the trap of focusing only inward, meeting the needs of those already in the building. But the call of the church has always been outward. If we're going to run to the brokenness in our cities, we must first ask: *Where is the brokenness?* And then we must go to it.

I often remind our church: We are the only organization in town that exists for the people who aren't here yet. That one statement sets the tone for our culture. (We'll discuss more about setting a good culture in chapter 8.) It creates guardrails to keep us from becoming self-centered or inwardly focused. It reminds us that our mission isn't about preserving comfort—it's about pursuing people.

And here's the beautiful part: as we faithfully focus on the needs *outside* the church, God consistently takes care of the needs *inside* the church. This isn't just a leadership principle—it's a biblical one.

"Give, and it will be given to you. A good measure, pressed down, shaken together and running over, will be poured into your lap" (Luke 6:38). When Jesus taught this principle, He wasn't just speaking about financial generosity—He was describing a posture of the heart. A church that gives itself away in service, generosity, and mission will always find itself in the overflow of God's provision. But the question is: *Can we see the need?*

In Luke 10, Jesus tells the story of the Good Samaritan, a man who saw what others refused to see. A priest and a Levite walked past a broken man bleeding on the side of the road, not because they were evil but because they were spiritually blind. They had grown numb to suffering. They were doing "business as usual," hurrying to the next temple task, unaware that they were walking past a divine assignment.

That's what spiritual blindness does. It blinds us to the brokenness around us and to the blessings God wants to release *through* us when we stop, see, and serve.

But the Samaritan saw differently. He saw with *prophetic imagination*—the ability to envision healing where others only saw a hassle. He didn't just feel pity; he acted with compassion. And Jesus said, "Go and do likewise" (Luke 10:27).

When we run to the brokenness, it's not just strategy—it's obedience. And obedience always brings blessing and favor. That's what Luke 6:38 is pointing to: the generous life is the blessed life. When we give ourselves away to the hurting, the overlooked, and the forgotten, God pours back more than we could ever give.

IDENTIFY THE NEED

Let's be leaders who see the need. Let's be churches that refuse to walk past pain. And let's believe that every time we respond with obedience, God will respond with overflow.

When a church gives itself away—in service, in generosity, in mission—God always pours back more than enough. Running to the brokenness isn't just a strategy. It's obedience. And obedience always brings blessing and favor.

Here's the good news: you don't have to figure it all out on your own. You can:

1) Collaborate with local schools.
2) Collaborate with other local churches.

In *Rooting for Rivals*, Peter Greer and Chris Horst make a compelling case for kingdom collaboration. They challenge ministries to resist the urge to compete and instead embrace a spirit of generosity and partnership, believing that when one church wins, we all win.[6] That mindset has reshaped how I view the mission of the church. It's not about building bigger crowds or louder platforms. It's about building God's kingdom—together. That's exactly why we became a distribution site for Convoy of Hope.

 **IMPACT STARTS WITH PRESENCE. BUT PRESENCE STARTS WITH ASKING.**

---

6   Peter Greer and Chris Horst, *Rooting for Rivals: How Collaboration and Generosity Increase the Impact for Leaders, Charities, and Churches* (Minneapolis, MN: Bethany House Publishers, July 3, 2018).

Today, we have more than thirty churches and nonprofits that regularly come to our campus to pick up free food and essential supplies, through our partnership with Convoy of Hope. Many of these are smaller congregations that don't have the infrastructure or resources to receive large-scale product donations on their own. But by sharing what's been entrusted to us, we're helping them reach the brokenness in *their* communities. We're not just stocking our own shelves—we're helping stock theirs. And that's what the church should be known for. When we choose collaboration over competition, we multiply the impact. When we root for our "rivals," we break down unnecessary walls and become the unified Body of Christ that Jesus prayed for in John 17. And when we run to the brokenness together, the healing comes faster, the hope goes further, and the glory goes to God—not to us.

Let's be churches that cheer each other on. Let's be leaders who hold our blessings with open hands. Because when we all bring what we have to the table, there's always more than enough to meet the need.

1) **Collaborate with local businesses.**

Recently, while eating lunch, I had the opportunity to pray for the owner of the restaurant where I was eating. As we talked, I recognized the brokenness in her life and even in her business. And here's what I've learned: when you begin to openly and compassionately engage with people about the areas of brokenness in their lives, organizations, or businesses, it creates an incredibly powerful point of connection. God often uses those moments—and blesses them with unexpected favor.

IDENTIFY THE NEED

2) **Collaborate with your local government.**

One of the most powerful ways a church can impact its city is by engaging the very people who shape it—including those in public office. As pastors and ministry leaders, we must be willing to work alongside government officials, even when we don't agree with them on every issue. Why? Because the mission of God is bigger than our personal politics or preferences.

Local leaders—mayors, city council members, school board officials, department heads—often carry a deep awareness of the brokenness in their communities. They hear the cries for help, see the budget shortfalls, and shoulder the weight of unmet needs. But rarely do they hear from the Church, saying, *"We're here to help."*

When we humble ourselves and ask, *"What do you need?"* we communicate that we're not just interested in growing our church—we're committed to serving our city. The needs we uncover may not be glamorous. They may not align perfectly with our ministry plans. But if we're serious about running to the brokenness, we must be willing to roll up our sleeves and work with those already fighting on the front lines.

It starts with presence. And presence begins with asking the right people—even the ones we may not always see eye to eye with—for the sake of the Kingdom.

One of the best things my parents taught me was to put myself in someone else's shoes. When I started LifeBridge, I applied that principle to our local government leaders. I would ask myself:

What pressure are they facing?
What keeps them up at night?

How can our church come alongside them and help?
This simple mindset opened the door for incredible favor.

OUR FIRST BIG DOOR: SAROYAN ELEMENTARY
In 2005, as we prepared to officially launch our church, we had no location. We were excited about a local elementary school, and I confidently met with the principal—only to be flat-out rejected. He had hosted churches before and had had bad experiences.

I left devastated.

But one of our core team members suggested we do something bold—something biblical. A Jericho March around the school. (See Joshua 6:1-20, where God brought down the walls of Jericho after Israel marched in obedience around the city for seven days.)

That weekend, our tiny core group of about fifteen people gathered in front of the school. No fanfare. No microphones. Just simple, humble obedience. We began to march and pray, asking God for favor and open doors.

As we walked those sidewalks and prayed over every classroom, every hallway, every child who would walk through those doors, something shifted—not in the natural but in the spiritual. We could feel it. There was a new sense of optimism and confidence in our team as if God had breathed fresh courage into our lungs. Somehow, some way, we believed God had heard our prayers and was going to honor our obedience. Even though the situation hadn't changed in the physical world, something had absolutely shifted in the spiritual realm.

IDENTIFY THE NEED

That moment solidified us. It knit our hearts together. We weren't just a group starting a church—we were a people chasing a promise.

The following Monday, I met the principal again. This time, I shared a new vision: "We won't just be here on Sundays. We want to help your school Monday through Saturday."

By the end of the meeting, God had softened his heart, and he gave us a chance, with one condition: if the teachers complained, they were out.

I asked him what his biggest need was. Without hesitation, he said, "A crossing guard."

So, for eighteen months, I put on an orange vest, stood out in the heat, and directed traffic, getting flipped off by impatient parents. It wasn't glamorous. But it was faithfulness in anonymity that God blessed. That small act opened the door to nearly two decades of partnership with our local schools, resulting in hundreds of thousands of dollars in in-kind donations and immeasurable kingdom impact. The teachers and the Parent Faculty Club came to love the partnership. We paid for teacher appreciation lunches (one of the best ways to make friends with a teacher!) and helped raise funds for classroom needs.

In fact, our presence became so meaningful that during one of the school's annual carnivals—a fundraiser *we* had helped support—the school turned around and gave *us* a generous financial donation. That's the kind of trust and favor that's possible when a church runs to the brokenness and chooses to serve with no strings attached.

In fact, when that principal was later promoted to a role at the district office, he said something I'll never forget. Upon his departure, he stated, "The best decision I ever made as a principal was allowing LifeBridge to meet at our school."

How did he go from a hard "no" to saying that allowing us in was the best decision he ever made?

Simple: we ran to the brokenness of the school.

Maybe your church is up against a wall right now. Maybe there's an opportunity in front of you that seems closed. Perhaps the key to breakthrough is this: run to the brokenness.

DON'T MISS THE HIDDEN NEEDS

You never know where the connection points will come from. That's why your church must stay alert, present, and available.

That one "yes" to serving as a crossing guard may have seemed small at the time, but it helped shape who we are today. It was sweaty, thankless, and unimpressive. But that single act of obedience—responding to a simple, overlooked need—unlocked something far greater. It opened the door to nearly two decades of partnership with our local schools. And it wasn't just about access to a building; it was about access to people's hearts.

That one "yes" led to thousands more. Yeses that looked like backpacks filled with supplies. Yeses that looked like food on empty tables. Yeses that looked like clothing for new immigrants and safe shelter for the unhoused. And most importantly, yeses that looked like lives surrendered to Jesus.

That one "yes" didn't just build partnership—it reshaped our posture as a church. We began to see that when we

IDENTIFY THE NEED

respond to the obvious, tangible needs in front of us, God often reveals the hidden, eternal ones too. When we say yes to serving, He opens doors we never imagined and entrusts us with influence we never sought.

So, at LifeBridge, we have a simple rule: if a school or community leader asks for help, we say YES. And because of this commitment, the public schools now call us when they have a need, much like they would call a first responder.

A few years ago, I got a call from the principal of one of our local middle schools. The tone in her voice was urgent—but the request? It caught me off guard.

"Would your church be able to provide a bicycle for one of our students?"

It wasn't Christmas. It wasn't part of any planned outreach. It was just a regular weekday in May.

She went on to explain that one of their students had recently had her bike stolen, and that bike was her only way to get to school. Her single mom couldn't afford a replacement, and now the girl was missing class. She was falling behind.

"I know your church gives out bikes to kids every Christmas," the principal said. "And I wasn't sure who else to call. . . . but I figured I'd ask."

She was referring to our annual Christmas bicycle giveaway, one of our most joy-filled events of the year. Every December, we rally our church and community to provide bikes to children who otherwise wouldn't receive one. It's become a beloved tradition—and apparently, our reputation had stuck.

RUN TO THE BROKENNESS

For a moment, I hesitated. Everything in me wanted to respond logically—"I'm sorry, we don't have bikes just sitting in storage." And I almost said that.

But then the Holy Spirit whispered, *You never say no to the schools.*

That simple phrase gripped my heart.

So, instead of declining, I responded, "Let me see what we can do."

I walked straight into our youth pastor's office and said, "Grab your truck. We're going to Walmart."

That afternoon, we rolled out of the parking lot with a brand-new bike—one we hadn't planned for, hadn't budgeted for... but one that would become a vehicle for so much more than just transportation.

The principal arranged for us to deliver the bike personally to the student and her mother in the school office. When we walked in holding that bright blue bike, both burst into tears.

In that moment, they weren't just receiving a bicycle.

They were receiving dignity.

They were receiving hope.

As they thanked us through their tears, they opened up about their struggle—about how they were barely making ends meet, about how this bike was more than just a gift; it was a lifeline.

I asked if I could pray for them, and right there in the school office, I laid hands on that mother and daughter and asked God to meet them in their brokenness.

Three weeks later, they showed up at our church.

And that Sunday, both gave their lives to Jesus.

They would have never walked through the doors of our church on their own. But they *rode* in on the ripple effect of a bicycle. A simple "yes" opened the door to transformation.

That call from the school wasn't just a request for a bike. It was a divine appointment.

It was one more reminder that when a church becomes known in its city as a *first responder* to brokenness, needs will come knocking. And when you say yes to those needs, you never know who might meet Jesus on the other side.

Never underestimate the power of one humble, faithful yes.

A CHURCH LIKE A FIRST RESPONDER

You've heard me say often that the church should be as vital to a community as our first responders, that if we closed our doors tomorrow, the city would feel it. For one student and her family, that became a living reality.

When her family first immigrated to the United States, they arrived with almost nothing—no furniture, no food, no warm clothing, and no understanding of the English language. Like many who pursue the American Dream, they found the barriers overwhelming. Navigating paperwork, housing, and employment while trying to raise a family in a foreign land felt impossible.

But that's when something extraordinary happened.

The local school district saw their need and paid for this student and others to take a bus to our thrift store—not just once but every week. What began as a simple effort to provide clothing and food quickly became something more. They met our team. They met Renee, one of our volunteers, who didn't speak Spanish but stood faithfully by their side every Saturday. And soon, they began attending our Sunday services. The mother started coming to our Spanish service, and her daughter—curious and determined—began attending the English services, even when she didn't yet understand the language.

Over time, something shifted.

She saw our youth director visit her school. She began to show up to youth group on Wednesdays. She went to summer camp, and it was there that she encountered the Holy Spirit in a life-changing way. She came home and got baptized. She gave her life fully to Jesus. And not long after, she stepped into youth ministry as a volunteer.

Today, she's a leader in our church, not just a recipient of help but a conduit of hope.

"I know I have someone to fight my battles," she told us. "And now I get to be that for someone else. The love I received—I get to give that away."

This is why we do what we do. This is why a thrift store is more than a store. It's why groceries are more than groceries. It's why a preschool, a nonprofit, or an event center can become a sacred space. When a church chooses to run to the brokenness—not just spiritually but practically—it becomes a first responder in the deepest sense.

And as this story reminds us, community is what makes the difference. Hope, dignity, and salvation don't always begin in the sanctuary. Sometimes, they start with a backpack of clothes and a warm smile on a Saturday afternoon.

PRAY FOR GOD'S FAVOR

One of the great miracles of ministry is that you will never have all the resources you need. But when you step out in faith, God will supply.

Psalm 90:17 says, "May the favor of the Lord our God rest on us; establish the work of our hands for us." This verse is both a prayer and a promise. It reminds us that while we may plan, build, and labor, it's *God* who ultimately establishes and sustains what we do. The Hebrew word for "establish" in this context means to *make firm, secure, or lasting*. It's the difference between good ideas and God-ordained impact.

At LifeBridge, we've seen this truth come alive again and again. We didn't manufacture favor—God gave it. And He didn't just sprinkle it on our dreams—He *established* them.

- **God brought a grant writer to our team**, not because we were out recruiting but because He knew what was coming and positioned the right person in the right seat at the right time.
- **God opened funding sources** from state and local government to private foundations to social enterprise opportunities we never could have predicted.
- **God stirred hearts to give generously** through people inside and outside the church who felt compelled to invest in the mission because they saw the fruit.

This verse is a reminder that the success of kingdom work isn't about striving harder; it's about surrendering deeper. When we align with God's heart, run to the brokenness, and remain faithful in the unseen and the unglamorous, *His* favor rests on us.

And when God's favor rests on a church, ordinary efforts produce extraordinary outcomes. That's what we've experienced. From a small group marching around a school in prayer, to a food pantry that became a community lifeline, to preschool programs and event centers that help fund the mission—all of it has been established not by our hands alone but by the hand of God.

PASTOR, FAVOR DOESN'T COME BECAUSE WE SEEK IT— IT COMES BECAUSE WE SERVE PEOPLE WELL.

So, as you pursue the work God is calling your church to do, dream big, yes, but pray even bigger. Ask God to establish the work of *your* hands. His favor will take your faithfulness further than you ever imagined.

Years later, after a funeral for one of our beloved volunteers, the mayor of our city approached me. I simply asked him, "What's the greatest need in our city, and how can we help?" His answer: housing. At the time, I never imagined that LifeBridge would become the catalyst for a $22 million affordable housing project in Fresno. But that's what happens when you ask, listen, and obey. God takes small prayers and turns them into massive miracles. Ephesians 3:20 says, "Now to him who is able to do immeasurably more than all we ask or imagine."

One of the most beautiful surprises of leadership is that when you faithfully serve the broken, favor follows.

I remember the day the mayor told me, "If we had more churches like LifeBridge, Fresno wouldn't need a police department." We were later praised by a city council member—someone who typically doesn't align closely with churches—for opening our thrift store as a warming center during a dangerous cold snap.

Pastor, favor doesn't come because we seek it—it comes because we serve people well.

BE A HUB, NOT JUST A BUILDING

My friend John B. in Surprise, Arizona, leads a mobile church that spends $400,000 every year hosting a five-day Christmas in the Park event because his city needs places for people to gather. Over 40,000 people attend.

People criticize him for not saving that money for a building. But John says, "What matters more is that we're a city-shaper church."

Your church becomes a hub based on how well you run to the brokenness in your city, not how fancy your facilities are. When you ask God to break your heart for what breaks His—and when you dare to act on that burden—miracles follow.

APPLICATION

You can't run to the brokenness if you don't first recognize where the brokenness is. As leaders, we must develop spiritual eyes—not just to see what's obvious, but to discern what's underneath. Many churches miss their greatest opportunities for impact simply because they aren't looking in the right places ... or asking the right people

Here are some practical ways to begin identifying the true needs in your community:

- **Ask those who know.** Schedule intentional conversations with school principals, local business owners, nonprofit leaders, and even civic officials. Ask them: *What's one major need in our neighborhood that you wish someone would do something about?* Then listen without judgment or agenda.
- **Get out of the building.** You can't see the pain of your city from a church office. Walk the streets. Volunteer in a school. Sit with people in your church who are struggling. You will begin to see gaps that aren't always visible on Sunday mornings.
- **Look beyond the surface.** Not all brokenness looks the same. Some needs are loud and visible (like hunger or homelessness), while others are quiet and hidden (like isolation, mental health, or abuse). Pray for the kind of spiritual awareness the Good Samaritan had—a willingness to *see* and *stop*.
- **Equip your leaders to be need identifiers.** Train your staff and volunteers to constantly ask: *Where is the brokenness in this room, in this meeting, in this moment?* Culture shifts when your people start spotting needs without being prompted.

> **Invite God to expand your vision.** Ask the Holy Spirit to help you develop prophetic imagination—not just to see what's broken, but to envision what could be redeemed. When you begin to see your city through God's eyes, you'll find that the needs around you become divine invitations, not interruptions.

REFLECTION

1) What brokenness or unmet need in your community have you overlooked?
2) Who can you ask—government leaders, schools, non-profits—to help you identify local needs?
3) How can you collaborate with other churches or businesses?
4) Where is God asking you to "just say yes" right now?
5) How can you cultivate a culture in your church that doesn't become numb to brokenness?

CHAPTER 4

RESPOND TO COMMUNITY CRISIS

How your church responds to crisis will either accelerate your influence or diminish it.

One of the greatest opportunities for your church to become the hub of your community is to step up when the community is going through a crisis. Nothing will increase your church's influence more than your ability to respond when no one else is stepping up. Even people who are opposed to God or the local church will often respect a church that shows up in times of real need.

I've seen this over and over: the brokenness in your community is a remarkable opportunity for groups that are often divided—churches, government agencies, non-profits, and businesses—to come together for a common cause. And what better organization to help lead that than the local church?

RUN TO THE BROKENNESS

RESPONDING TO THE BROKENNESS IN EVERY COMMUNITY: THE STORY OF RUBI

One of the most important lessons I've learned on this journey is that brokenness doesn't look the same in every zip code.

In some communities, it shows up in addiction, homelessness, and poverty. In others, it may take the form of hidden pain, grief, isolation, or unspoken trauma that lies just beneath the surface in otherwise well-resourced neighborhoods. But make no mistake: brokenness is everywhere. And God calls the church to run toward it, wherever it may be.

A powerful example of this comes from a good friend of mine, a pastor whose church is located in one of the more affluent areas of his city. On December 16, 2024, a tragedy rocked their community. A teacher and a fourteen-year-old student named Rubi were killed during an act of violence at a private Christian school. Several others were injured. And while this school wasn't officially affiliated with his church, many of their youth were present that day. Some were just feet from the trauma. Others had deep connections to the families affected.

The days that followed were filled with heartbreak but also opportunity.

Their church stepped up in love, bringing lasagnas, flowers, and prayer. They hosted indoor prayer vigils, partnered in fundraisers, and offered quiet, steady support. But they didn't stop there. They kept asking the question we all must ask when brokenness shows up in our community: *How do we keep showing up when the headlines fade?*

That question became the seed of something extraordinary.

RESPOND TO COMMUNITY CRISIS

Rubi wasn't just a name in a tragic news story. She was a joyful, Jesus-loving teen who looked forward to attending *Lifest* (a large Christian music festival) every summer. During her memorial service, Bob Lenz of Life Promotions heard her story and was moved to tears. Through a divine connection with Rubi's family, a conversation emerged that would soon become a movement.

Rubi's mother, Jen, said through tears, "If more people could hear Rubi's story and come to Jesus, it wouldn't take the pain away—but at least something good would come from it."

That desire to bring purpose from pain ignited the Extend the Impact initiative.

In Rubi's honor, Lifest committed to printing and distributing 10,000 free tickets—gifts of grace—designed to be handed out to students, neighbors, coworkers, and anyone who might not step into a church but might be open to hearing the gospel through music. These tickets, bearing Rubi's legacy, have become more than entry passes. They are invitations to encounter hope. Seeds of healing planted in memory of a life that loved Jesus.

And the church, my friend's church, helped lead the charge.

They didn't let their zip code determine their level of urgency. They didn't dismiss the grief because it wasn't their school. They stepped into the pain, honored the life lost, and found a way to bring redemption in the midst of tragedy.

This is what it looks like to run to the brokenness.

You don't have to be in a high-crime neighborhood to find broken hearts.

You don't have to have a food bank to serve those who are spiritually hungry.

You don't have to be located in the "rough part of town" to see lives changed.

Brokenness is everywhere, and so is opportunity.

The question for every church is: *Will we run to it?*

That choice is revealed in how we respond. Here are a few ways we can lead with courage and clarity when it matters most.

Look for the Opportunity in the Crisis

The natural tendency in a crisis is to pull inward—to protect ourselves, our families, our buildings, and our people. And there's nothing wrong with ensuring your church family is safe. But the churches that become hubs of hope are the ones that ask: *How can we serve others, not just ourselves, in this moment?*

When COVID-19 hit in March 2020, I faced the unthinkable as a pastor: we had to shut down Sunday services. I remember the feelings of fear and despair, wondering how we would survive financially without cash reserves and whether the church could endure.

A spiritual mentor challenged me with a phrase that became a lifeline: "Look for the opportunity in the obstacle."

At first, I didn't want to hear it. But I went into our sanctuary and prayed, "God, if You can use us to bring hope and help during this dark time, show us how."

When I left the sanctuary, I looked across the street at Costco and saw a long line of people anxious, desperate, and worried about running out of basic supplies. That moment sparked an idea:

What if we could counter the pandemic of fear with a pandemic of hope?

So, we set up signs reading "Curbside Prayer" outside our church, right across from Costco. As people waited in lines, they saw our young adults waving signs, calling out, "Curbside prayer! Step right up!"

To our amazement, people came for prayer, many in tears, anxious for their families. Soon, local media covered the story, and our prayer line stretched over a mile.

James 5:16 reminds us, "The prayer of a righteous person is powerful and effective."

This effort made our church a beacon of calm during a season of fear and isolation. The church parking lot became a place of healing. And many people who had never stepped inside a church suddenly experienced the peace and love of Christ—in their cars with tears streaming down their faces.

As we prayed with people, we realized one consistent request: "We don't have enough food."

Our hearts were broken. I went into the sanctuary again and prayed, "Lord, we can't use this space for Sunday gatherings right now. We have this beautiful building, and it's so sad that we can't use it to gather! What can we do, Lord?"

And I heard God speak clearly: "Turn the sanctuary into a storehouse."

That word from God would forever change the trajectory of our church.

We began asking our congregation to donate groceries. As word spread, demand outgrew our resources, so we reached out to the local food bank. Despite the sanctuary not meeting normal warehouse standards, they worked with us to make it happen.

Within weeks, we became the first organization in our community to host a drive-through grocery giveaway, minimizing contact and maximizing help. We weren't just distributing food; we were distributing dignity, peace, and the love of Christ.

Isaiah 58:7 speaks directly to this calling: "Is it not to share your food with the hungry and to provide the poor wanderer with shelter—when you see the naked, to clothe them?"

By Christmas that year, we were running out of money to keep the feeding program going. I remember standing by the sanctuary wall during the grocery giveaway, overwhelmed, crying out: *God, You have to do a miracle!*

Shortly after, we were awarded a $500,000 federal grant to sustain the program—an unmistakable answer to prayer.

Philippians 4:19 says, "And my God will meet all your needs according to the riches of his glory in Christ Jesus." While this verse reminds us that God is our Provider, the reality that many pastors face today tells a different story, at least on the surface.

According to a report from Barna, only 27 percent of pastors in 2023 said their church's financial health was excellent, down from 43 percent before the pandemic.[7] Financial instability has led many churches to scale back or eliminate

---

7 Barna Group, *The State of Pastors*, Volume 2. Ventura, CA: Barna Group, 2023.

programs entirely. But your church can be different because the same God who fed thousands with five loaves and two fish still multiplies what we offer in faith (Matthew 14:13-21).

Be the First to Respond

One of the most humbling surprises in our journey came the day we were honored with the Frontline Community Hero Award. It happened at the Fresno County State of the County breakfast in front of an audience of over 700 of the region's top business and government leaders. LifeBridge was one of just four organizations recognized, alongside the Nurses Association, the Air National Guard, and the fire department.

GOD DESIGNED THE CHURCH TO BE THE FIRST TO RESPOND.

To be honest, I felt out of place. Standing there representing a church among these high-profile institutions was surreal. But then the county leaders said something I'll never forget: "LifeBridge was the first to respond to creatively providing for our community before any government organization stood up to meet the need."

That one sentence brought me back to a hot August day years earlier when I first arrived in Fresno with a dream—a vision that one day, the church we planted would be seen as essential to the life and well-being of the community, as essential as the first responders in our community. Not just a place for Sunday services but a trusted presence during crisis. That day, standing alongside military and medical heroes, I realized something powerful: God designed the church to be the first to respond. Not to wait for permission. Not to stand on the sidelines. But to run toward the brokenness with faith, compassion, and practical help. That award wasn't just an honor; it was confirmation. The church can be seen as vital again, as vital as the police, fire, and medical professionals. All it takes is obedience, courage, and a willingness to lead the way when others hesitate. The church can be the hub of your community. (Don't forget about Jesus's charge to us in Matthew 25:35-36.)

One of the most unforgettable moments that reminded me of this truth came when a man in our church named Michael approached me after a Sunday service, looking a little unsure but also deeply moved, and asked if he could invite a homeless woman named Cheryl to church.

"Pastor," he said, "there's a woman I met—her name's Cheryl. She's homeless. I feel like I should invite her to church. Is that okay?"

"Of course, it's okay," I said without hesitation. "That's who we are. We run to the brokenness."

You can preach about being a church that welcomes the hurting, but moments like that reveal whether it's embedded in your culture. Michael extended the invitation. Cheryl said yes.

The first Sunday she walked through our doors, everything changed, not just for her but for us. Her clothes were worn, her eyes carried the weight of life on the streets, and her story was written in pain. But from the moment she stepped inside, something beautiful happened. Our people rallied around her—no judgment, no awkward stares, just love. Just open arms. Just Jesus. That's the power of a church culture where broken people feel safe, seen, and welcomed. And that's why cultivating that kind of culture is not optional; it's essential.

 **THE CHURCH SHOULD BE THE FIRST TO RESPOND, NOT THE LAST RESORT.**

Week after week, Cheryl came back. And week after week, I watched her shoulders straighten a little more. Her eyes began to soften; her countenance began to change. And then, one Sunday morning during an altar call, she walked forward and gave her life to Christ.

Tears streamed down her face. The kind of tears that speak of surrender, of healing, of hope. The kind of tears that say, "I've come home."

But God wasn't done.

RUN TO THE BROKENNESS

About two months later, we rented out a local theater to show the film *Jesus Revolution*.[8] Cheryl showed up that night—but this time, she wasn't alone. She brought her husband, George. A man with one leg. A man who had battled homelessness and drug addiction for most of his life.

He shuffled into the theater that night with crutches and curiosity. He didn't know exactly what he was walking into. But God did.

As the credits rolled, I stood at the front of the theater and gave a simple invitation.

"If you want to give your life to Christ, stand to your feet."

There was a pause. Then movement.

George—this man with one leg—began to rise.

And as he did, he started to fall.

But before he could hit the floor, two members of our church, and our Spanish campus pastor rushed over and lifted him. They stood beside him, holding him up while the rest of the room bowed their heads in prayer.

That moment . . . that moment wrecked me.

A man with one leg stood for Jesus—and the body of Christ stood with him.

That's the kind of church I want to be. That's the kind of church we must be.

Today, Cheryl and George are no longer homeless. They have their own apartment. Cheryl has a job. And in a beautiful twist of redemption, she now volunteers in our outreach

---

[8] Jon Erwin and Brent McCorkle, *Jesus Revolution* (February 24, 2023; Nashville TN and Los Angeles, CA: Kingdom Story Company).

programs, ministering to homeless men and women battling the very demons that once tried to destroy her.

She's not just attending church—she's being the church.

When people ask me what it means to "run to the brokenness," I tell them this story because it's not just a story about Cheryl and George. It's a story about the gospel. It's a story about what happens when ordinary people, filled with an extraordinary God, choose to run toward the pain, not away from it. It's a story about what happens when the church does what Jesus always did—see the one, love the one, heal the one.

Because when we run to the brokenness, we discover the kingdom of God is already waiting there.

Empower Your Church to Respond

Your people want to be part of something meaningful. Don't underestimate the willingness of your congregation to show up, even in crisis.

Create simple ways for people to serve. Offer multiple levels of involvement, from prayer teams to packing boxes to delivering supplies.

Equip your people not just to survive but to serve.

Second Corinthians 9:12-13 says, "This service that you perform is not only supplying the needs of the Lord's people but is also overflowing in many expressions of thanks to God."

When a community is in crisis, the world watches to see who will show up. The church should be the first to respond, not the last resort. But running to the brokenness isn't just about emergency moments or national disasters—it's about building structures and systems that allow your church to be a consistent presence in people's pain. Sometimes, that looks like curbside prayer and food giveaways. Other times, it's a simple preschool program that opens a door none of us saw coming.

Earlier in this chapter, you read about Cheryl. Her journey to Jesus didn't start in a sanctuary—it started with a man named Michael, whose life turned around because he came to church for a preschool program. That preschool was a social enterprise—created to meet a real need in our city. And in doing so, it became a gateway for life transformation.

This is why the model matters—because when churches step outside their four walls, when we meet practical needs with purpose and compassion, we create access points for the gospel we never could have planned. And the ripple effects—like Cheryl's, Michael's, and George's stories—are what remind us that no act of service is wasted.

You don't need to have it all figured out. You just need to be willing to show up.

Crises will come—we can't avoid them. But we can choose how we respond. And when the local church steps up, the community takes notice.

When your church runs to the brokenness, whether in crisis or everyday struggle, you become the heartbeat of your community.

In the next chapter, we'll look at how to build partnerships with nonprofits, businesses, and civic leaders to sustain and multiply your outreach—because no church changes a city alone.

APPLICATION

Crisis has a way of revealing what's already true—about us, our churches, and our communities. When tragedy strikes or urgent needs arise, people don't turn to a website or mission statement. They turn to *people*. The question is: will your church be known as a place that runs toward the pain or retreats from it?

Here are practical ways to prepare and position your church to respond to crisis effectively:

- **Decide in advance who you are.** You don't rise to the occasion in crisis—you fall to the level of your preparation. Make it part of your church's identity to respond quickly, generously, and compassionately. Say it from the platform. Bake it into your culture.
- **Build relationships before you need them.** Crisis is not the time to start networking. Cultivate strong relationships with school administrators, city leaders, nonprofits, and emergency responders *before* something happens. Trust takes time—but it pays dividends in critical moments.
- **Don't underestimate small acts of presence.** Sometimes, the greatest gift your church can give in a crisis is simply showing up. A warm meal. A blanket. A quiet prayer. When we respond with love, not lectures, we open the door for deeper transformation.

- **Empower your team to say "yes."** When a principal calls about a student without a bike or a shelter asks for extra blankets, your team should feel empowered to act without jumping through endless approval processes. Create guardrails but trust your people to carry the vision.
- **Let faith lead, not fear.** It's easy to be overwhelmed by need—especially in moments of community-wide crisis. But remember: your job isn't to fix *everything*. Your job is to be obedient to the opportunities God *puts in front of you*. Say "yes" to what's in your hand, and trust Him for the rest.

REFLECTION

1) How has your church responded to past community crises?
2) What have you learned about God's provision during those seasons?
3) Where do you see potential opportunities for your church to lead in your city?
4) How can you prepare your leaders to be ready when the next crisis comes?
5) How might crisis response strengthen the reputation and witness of your church?
6) How can your church prepare now to respond in a future crisis?
7) Who in your church has skills or resources to help in a crisis?

8) What small steps can you take this year to partner with city leaders, schools, or nonprofits?
9) How will you help your congregation develop the mindset of serving outward even when facing internal challenges?

CHAPTER 5

BROKENNESS IS AN OPPORTUNITY

Pastor, your next great opportunity for ministry is not across the country, on a conference stage, or in a brand-new program.

Your next best opportunity is the brokenness right in your neighborhood.

Several years ago, while traveling through Egypt, I witnessed overwhelming poverty—people living in heartbreaking conditions. I remember standing there, stunned, as the Lord spoke clearly to my heart: "Run to the brokenness."

I have to admit, I wasn't always a fan of running to the brokenness. In fact, for a long time, I avoided it. I'd drive by someone unhoused, standing on the corner with a cardboard sign, and think, *Someone should really do something about that. Our city needs to do better.*

But deep down, I'd hear the voice of the Holy Spirit whispering, *What if that someone is you?*

And I'd argue back, *Lord, there's no way I can do something about this. What could I possibly do?*

What I didn't realize at the time was that God wasn't asking me to solve everything—He was asking me to *start*.

And over time, through steps of obedience I never would have predicted, He used me, someone who once looked away from brokenness, to help bring the most innovative and highest-funded affordable housing initiative in Fresno's history into being.

It still humbles me. What began with avoidance became alignment with God's heart.

If He can do that with me, He can do it with anyone.

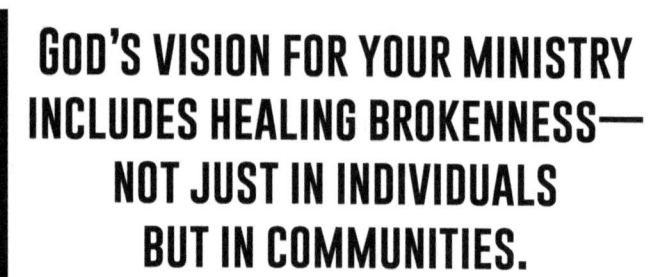

GOD'S VISION FOR YOUR MINISTRY INCLUDES HEALING BROKENNESS— NOT JUST IN INDIVIDUALS BUT IN COMMUNITIES.

Up to that moment, I realized I had often avoided the broken places. But as leaders, if we avoid the brokenness around us, we risk missing the very places where God wants to display His power and compassion.

BROKENNESS: THE LEADERSHIP LENS

As ministry leaders, we often pour our energy into systems, services, strategies, and Sunday mornings. But let me ask you:

Are you aware of the brokenness in your city?

Do you know the struggles your congregation is carrying?

Are you willing to move toward pain, rather than away from it?

There's a reason brokenness is central to the gospel:

God's vision for your ministry includes healing brokenness— not just in individuals but in communities.

When we, as leaders, model vulnerability and healing, we become the kind of people God can use to heal our cities.

In Matthew 8:1-3, we meet a man with leprosy—a social outcast, an untouchable, someone people crossed the street to avoid:

When Jesus came down from the mountainside, large crowds followed him. A man with leprosy came and knelt before him and said, "Lord, if you are willing, you can make me clean."

Jesus reached out his hand and touched the man. "I am willing," he said. "Be clean!" Immediately he was cleansed of his leprosy.

Pastor and ministry leader, Jesus never avoids the broken. We are called to lead our churches in the same way. Theologically, here's why this matters: God entered the brokenness of the world through Jesus to redeem it.

We lead people into brokenness because we follow a Savior who did the same.

As leaders, we are tempted to avoid messy, complex issues. But Jesus moved toward poverty, disease, injustice, and pain, not away. That's our model for ministry.

That kind of leadership doesn't happen by accident—it requires a posture of heart and a set of convictions that shape how we show up.

Leading Toward Brokenness Requires Desperation for Jesus

In ministry, it's easy to get desperate for the wrong things: growth, bigger budgets, better facilities, or more staff. But what if God is waiting for us to become desperate for *Him*? Desperate not for outcomes but for His presence. That kind of holy desperation doesn't begin with strategy—it begins with surrender.

In Matthew 8, a man with leprosy comes to Jesus with no religious standing, no medical solution, and no social status. All he has is desperation, and Jesus meets him with compassion and power. That's still true today.

When we stop pretending we have it all together and instead admit how much we need God, everything shifts. Every miracle in Scripture began with something broken. And every revival begins with a leader on their knees.

So, what does desperation for Jesus actually look like in the life of a leader? Here's where it starts:

- **Admitting our own brokenness as leaders**
- **Modeling humility and dependence on God**
- **Recognizing that in our churches and cities, something must change**

When you run toward the broken places in yourself and around you, you position yourself for a front-row seat to God's power.

The man in Matthew 8 had no religious or medical solution—only Jesus.

Every miracle in Scripture began with something broken:
- The paralyzed man (Mark 2)
- The blind man (John 9)
- Lazarus (John 11)

As a leader, if you want to see God's power at work, you must first acknowledge where things are broken.

Running to Brokenness Means Being Willing to Break the Mold

In Matthew 8, Jesus does the unthinkable—He touches a leper.

As leaders, we often feel pressure to play it safe, to follow what's predictable or acceptable in church culture. But sometimes, running to the brokenness will require you to:
- Cross uncomfortable boundaries
- Lead your team into unfamiliar territory
- Innovate when others stay stuck

Remember when we turned our sanctuary into a food distribution center during COVID-19? It wasn't part of anyone's strategic plan, but it allowed us to serve thousands of families. That act of "breaking the mold" led to us receiving the Frontline Community Hero Award from city leaders.

Pastor, are you willing to do what's uncomfortable to reach the broken?

RUN TO THE BROKENNESS

Leading Toward Brokenness Requires Movement

God honors movement. And leadership sets the pace for movement.

 **BROKENNESS IS THE OPPORTUNITY. AVOIDING IT MAY FEEL SAFE, BUT RUNNING TOWARD IT IS WHERE GOD'S POWER IS UNLEASHED.**

Think about the miracles in Scripture:
- **The man with the shriveled hand stretched it out.** *(Mark 3:1-6)*
- **The blind man went to wash.** *(John 9:6-7)*
- **The centurion father sought out Jesus.** *(Matthew 8:5-13)*
- **Mary and Martha sent word to Jesus for Lazarus.** *(John 11:1-3)*

Each of these miracles began with a step of faith, often from a place of deep brokenness and desperation.

As a pastor, you are the lead mover in your church. If you want your people to run toward brokenness, you must go first:
- Walk the streets of your city.
- Meet with government or nonprofit leaders.
- Bring broken stories into the light from the pulpit.

When you move, your people follow.

Pastor, brokenness is the opportunity. Avoiding it may feel safe, but running toward it is where God's power is unleashed.

BROKENNESS IS AN OPPORTUNITY

As you step into the brokenness of your city, you will soon discover you can't do it alone. In the next chapter, we'll explore how to build partnerships with nonprofits, city leaders, and businesses to multiply your church's impact.

APPLICATION

- Acknowledge your own brokenness. Your team needs to see a pastor who's honest about his own wounds and dependent on God.
- Call out brokenness in your city. Use your platform to name injustice, poverty, addiction, isolation, and despair.
- Move toward brokenness with practical action. Start small: partner with a local school, offer counseling scholarships, or create a benevolence team.
- Celebrate every win. Tell the stories of breakthrough in staff meetings, board meetings, and from the stage.

REFLECTION

1) Where do you see brokenness in your congregation that you've been avoiding?
2) What brokenness in your city or neighborhood have you not engaged with?
3) How can you lead your team to think innovatively about ministry to the broken?
4) What bold step can you take this month to move toward the pain in your community?
5) Where are you personally in need of Jesus's healing so you can lead with greater compassion?

CHAPTER 6

CREATING THE RIGHT CULTURE

Pastor and leader, one of the most important things you will ever build in your church is culture.

You can have the right mission, sharp systems, and a beautiful building—but if the culture is wrong, none of it will last. Culture answers the question: "What kind of people are we becoming?"

I'm currently part of the Sam Chand Leadership Institute, learning alongside other pastors across Southern California. One of the biggest takeaways for me has been this truth: when you change your culture, you change everything.[9] One of the highest callings that we have as leaders in our church is to consistently challenge people to change their habits to be holy. This sometimes can be a difficult process, and perhaps a little painful; in fact, culture is one of the most overlooked keys to long-term church health. But if God can use you and

---
[9] Sam Chand, *Change Your Culture, Change Everything: The Leader's Guide to Organizational Transformation* (Stockbridge, GA: Sam Chand Leadership Institute, 2017).

your church to change the habits of individual's lives, it can transform your church and your community.

In this chapter, I want to challenge you to build a culture that does what comes unnaturally—run toward brokenness.

 **IF YOU CHANGE THE CULTURE, YOU CAN CHANGE EVERYTHING.**

You can have great programs, a clear mission, and a talented team—but if the culture is unhealthy, it will hold everything back.

Culture changes everything.

This applies to your church, your family, your staff, and your ministry. If you change the feel of the environment— the way people think, interact, and behave—you can unlock growth, health, and transformation.

WHAT IS CULTURE?

Culture is simply this: your habits create your values, and your values shape your culture.

You can say you value family time, but if you're never home, you don't.

You can say you value prayer, but if you never pray, you don't.

You can say you value outreach, but if you never engage the lost, you don't.

CREATING THE RIGHT CULTURE

It's not just what we say—it's what we do that builds culture. As Jesus said in Matthew 7:17 and 20 (NLT): "A good tree produces good fruit, and a bad tree produces bad fruit... just as you can identify a tree by its fruit, you can identify people by their actions."

Years ago, when our daughter Cara first began learning how to drive, I had the privilege (and stress!) of teaching her. She was excited, nervous, and ready to hit the road. But what I didn't realize at the time was how much the experience would teach *me*—about culture, leadership, and the power of example.

You see, before Cara was old enough to drive, I had picked up a few bad driving habits. I'd speed here and there. Occasionally roll through a stop sign. I justified it by telling myself I had a lot to accomplish. I was always rushing from one meeting to the next, and if I could shave off a few minutes by pressing the gas pedal a little harder, why not?

Without realizing it, I had created a culture—one that made me feel like every time I got behind the wheel, I was playing Mario Kart. Other cars weren't fellow drivers. . . . they were obstacles in my way. Slowing me down. Delaying my purpose.

That "every once in a while" habit? It became a way of life. And that way of life? It started shaping my daughter.

(Which is exactly why we never put LifeBridge bumper stickers on our cars—probably for the best!)

Then, one day, it hit me.

Cara was fifteen, newly permitted, and riding in the front seat with me. I was running late for a meeting with a new visitor at church—someone I really wanted to make a good impression on. As usual, I put the pedal to the metal.

And then came the voice from the passenger seat: "Daddy, you shouldn't speed."

I laughed nervously and said, "Why not, baby?"

She looked at me—wide-eyed, serious—and said, "Because I'm learning how to drive from you. And if you keep speeding, I'll think that's okay. When I get my license, I might get a speeding ticket... or worse, I could get into an accident."

I was wrecked.

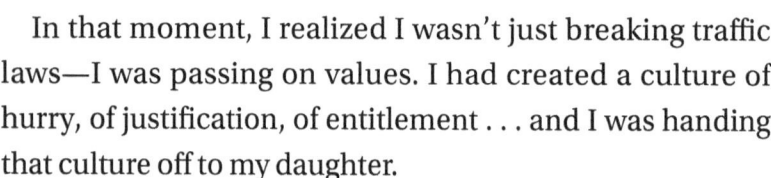

> YOU MAY HAVE FORMED A HABIT THAT'S QUIETLY SHAPING A VALUE, AND THAT VALUE MAY BE FORMING A CULTURE.

In that moment, I realized I wasn't just breaking traffic laws—I was passing on values. I had created a culture of hurry, of justification, of entitlement... and I was handing that culture off to my daughter.

I looked at her and said, "You're right, Cara. Daddy shouldn't do this. I'm sorry—and I won't do it anymore."

That was a turning point for me. Because culture isn't just what we say—it's what we do consistently. And whether we recognize it or not, we are always creating culture: in our homes, our churches, our businesses, and our relationships.

You may have formed a habit that's quietly shaping a value, and that value may be forming a culture.

And here's the hard truth: it's possible to be in a toxic culture and not even realize it.

Today, I want to challenge you to take inventory. Parents, pastors, business leaders—we are the cultural architects of our environments. We are shaping what feels "normal" for the people around us.

Right now, you are creating a culture, whether you realize it or not!

The question is: *What kind of culture will you pass on to the next generation, and how will that shape your church?*

HOW'S THE CULTURE IN YOUR CHURCH?

Let me ask you, pastor:

How's the culture in your home?

How's the culture on your team?

How's the culture in your church?

Maybe you've worked in a place where you loved the job but dreaded the environment. The mission was great, but the people were negative, gossipy, or divisive. The problem wasn't the job—it was the culture.

You can have a clear vision, solid preaching, and passionate worship—but if you don't change the culture, you won't change the outcome.

I grew up in a home that didn't value education or growth. It was a rough environment. I wasn't encouraged to dream or believe I could become much. But something shifted when I left home to attend North Central University in Minneapolis, Minnesota.

 **GOD CAN PLANT YOU IN A NEW ENVIRONMENT AND GROW IN YOU A DIFFERENT KIND OF FRUIT.**

The summer of 1995 changed my life forever. I wanted to intern with Gary Grogan, aka Papa G—one of the most respected pastors in the Midwest. His church, Stone Creek Church in Urbana, Illinois, was a flagship ministry in our movement.

I was terrified when I approached him after a chapel service. "Pastor Grogan, you don't know me, but I'd love to intern with you this summer." He kindly but firmly said no: the church was in a tough financial season.

I was crushed. Every message I'd absorbed from my childhood—"You're not good enough. You'll never make it. You're not talented enough."—came rushing back. I went back to my dorm, devastated, and began to pray.

That night, during another service, I felt God telling me, "Ask again."

I argued with God—I didn't want to look foolish—but eventually, I obeyed. After the service, I tapped Pastor Grogan on the shoulder and said, "I know you said no earlier, but I really feel like God is asking me to intern with you."

This time, he paused and said, "I'll talk to the elders and let you know."

Two weeks later, I got the call—I was accepted.

That summer marked the first time I experienced a healthy culture. Papa G took me under his wing. He taught me about leadership, humility, and service, including making me iron his clothes and clean toilets! I learned that real ministry is built on servanthood, not status.

I am who I am today, largely because I was pulled into a healthier culture.

You are not stuck in the culture you came from. God can plant you in a new environment and grow in you a different kind of fruit.

LEADERS ARE CULTURAL ARCHITECTS

As a pastor or ministry leader, you are the cultural architect.

Just like an architect draws blueprints for a building, you design the blueprint for how your family, your team, and your church operate. The structure may be spiritual, emotional, and relational, rather than made of wood and stone, but make no mistake—you are building something.

If you don't shape culture intentionally:

1) **Routine will shape it for you.**

Culture doesn't drift toward health—it drifts toward comfort. If we're not proactive, we'll default to what's easy, not what's best.

At one point in our church's early years, we noticed that staff meetings were starting to feel . . . flat. People showed up, went through the motions, and rushed back to their to-do lists. We weren't praying together, celebrating wins, or dreaming about the future. No one meant for it to happen—we had just slipped into a routine. That routine started shaping our culture. It took an intentional reset (and a few hard conversations) to inject life and vision back into the space.

Routine is a terrible architect. If you're not designing the culture you want, routine will build one you won't like.

2) **Complaining voices will shape it for you.**

The loudest voices in the room are not always the healthiest. But if they're not addressed, they can begin to steer the tone, priorities, and expectations of your culture.

Years ago, we had a few vocal members of the congregation who didn't like the way we were reaching unchurched people, from allowing guys to wear hats in service to the music being "too loud." Their criticism wasn't just personal preference—it started shaping how others viewed the church. People began walking on eggshells, second-guessing outreach efforts, and silencing creativity out of fear of criticism.

If you don't address complaining voices with clarity and courage, those voices will begin to lead your culture without ever having a position on the org chart.

3) **Unhealthy behaviors will shape it for you.**
Culture is what you allow, not just what you say. If unaddressed behaviors go unchecked—gossip, lateness, apathy, disunity—they will become the norm.

 ## CULTURE IS TOO IMPORTANT TO LEAVE TO CHANCE.

We once had a team member who consistently showed up late to Sunday setup. We joked about it at first—"That's just how they are!"—but soon, others started to follow suit. Before we knew it, half the team was dragging in late, and excellence was slipping. It wasn't a scheduling issue. It was a culture issue. We had unintentionally communicated, *Excellence doesn't matter here.*

What you tolerate becomes what you teach, even though it may be unintentional!

Bottom line: If you don't shape the culture of your church, someone else will. And if you're not shaping it with vision, it will be shaped by whatever is most convenient, loudest, or left unchecked.

So, lead intentionally. Culture is too important to leave to chance.

That's why Proverbs 29:18 (KJV) says, "Where *there is* no vision, the people perish." When leaders fail to cast and protect vision, the culture drifts—and often toward dysfunction.

Pastor, the day-to-day chaos of ministry—the broken AC, the last-minute crises, the urgent texts—will pull you off course unless you stay laser-focused on building a healthy culture. The apostle Paul reminded the early church leaders of their role when he wrote in 1 Corinthians 14:40: "But everything should be done in a fitting and orderly way." A healthy culture doesn't just happen; it is cultivated and protected with intention.

I also like to frame it this way: the leadership team of a church are the cultural gatekeepers. They are the ones who allow a culture to either flourish in the Spirit or drift away from what God intended it to be. One of the most difficult jobs of ministry leaders is maintaining a healthy culture over the long haul.

Galatians 6:9 encourages us in this endeavor: "Let us not grow weary in doing good, for at the proper time we will reap a harvest if we do not give up." Culture work is slow, persistent work, but it yields kingdom fruit that lasts.

As you lead, don't just ask, "What are we doing?" Ask, "What kind of people are we becoming?" That question will guide your blueprint and help you build a culture that honors God, attracts His presence, and motivates your congregation to run to the brokenness.

Some of you reading this are first-generation Christians. You're trying to break cycles your parents never broke—cycles of anger, addiction, chaos, poverty, or faithlessness.

My parents, thankfully, came to faith later in life. But early on, I had to decide:

Will I carry forward the old culture I was raised in, or will I build a new one?

If you want to break the cycle:
- You must behave differently.
- You must think differently.
- You must model something better.

It's hard—but it's worth it.

BUILDING HEALTHY HABITS AND CORE VALUES

At LifeBridge, we've learned that culture isn't just something you *teach*—it's something you *embody*. It flows not just from the vision we cast but from the people we entrust with leadership. Whether it's a staff hire or a key volunteer position, we know that each person will either reinforce or undermine the culture we're building. That's why we take seriously the process of identifying individuals who reflect the kind of values that align with the heart of our mission.

In fact, we've developed a framework we now use to guide those decisions, born out of prayer, experience, and insight from the book *The Ideal Team Player*.[10] We've contextualized and expanded that wisdom for our unique church culture, identifying seven traits we believe are essential to shaping and sustaining a healthy ministry environment:

1) Dependence on God. We look for people whose strength doesn't come from mere talent but from a

---

[10] Patrick M. Lencioni, *The Ideal Team Player: How to Recognize and Cultivate The Three Essential Virtues* (Hoboken, NJ: Jossey-Bass, 2016).

posture of surrender. Dependence on God anchors our purpose and gives clarity in decision-making, especially under pressure. It fuels integrity and reminds us we're not building our own kingdom—we're building His (Proverbs 3:5-6).

2) Self-Awareness. A healthy team member knows their strengths but also their blind spots. Self-awareness fosters humility, emotional intelligence, and teachability—qualities that are critical when navigating the complexities of ministry. As Romans 12:3 says, we are to think of ourselves with sober judgment.

3) Drive (or Hunger). Ministry takes grit. We look for individuals with a holy ambition—those who take initiative, bring energy, and pursue excellence not for ego but for impact (Colossians 3:23). These are the people who don't just fulfill a job description—they push the mission forward.

4) Humility. Great leaders don't need to be the loudest in the room. They serve quietly, lift others up, and deflect the credit. Humility keeps our egos in check and our hearts aligned with Jesus's model of servant leadership (Philippians 2:3-5).

5) Resilience. Ministry is not for the faint of heart. There will be criticism, loss, failure, and fatigue. Resilient team members have the emotional strength to bounce back, the spiritual grounding to endure, and the determination to keep showing up—no matter what (Galatians 6:9).

6) Adaptability. In a fast-changing world, and especially in innovative ministry, rigidity will break you. Adaptable people lean into change. They pivot without panic. They hold plans loosely and trust God deeply (Isaiah 43:19).
7) Sense of Humor. Yes, this made our list. Ministry can be heavy—but it shouldn't always feel heavy. People who laugh easily, who don't take themselves too seriously, who bring joy into the room—they make the work lighter and the journey more enjoyable (Proverbs 17:22). A cheerful heart is indeed good medicine.

When you prioritize people who embody these values, you don't just fill roles—you build culture. You create a team that's not only effective but spiritually healthy. And in the long run, that kind of team culture will shape your church more than any program ever could.

WHY HABITS MATTER
CULTURE STARTS WITH YOU

The culture of your church will never be healthier than the soul of its leaders.

In chapter 5, I shared the story of when my wife and I noticed abandoned shopping carts all over town when we first arrived in Fresno. To locals, this was normal. To us, it was a visible sign of neglect and brokenness. Instead of ignoring it, we gathered a small team, drove the streets, and started returning carts. That small act shaped something deep in our church: we will not be a church that ignores what's broken, and we will not be leaders who ignore the brokenness in our own lives.

When you model honesty about your own brokenness—financial, emotional, relational, spiritual—you open the door for a culture of healing.

Here are just a couple of ways you can model brokenness. Ask yourself:
Where do I need to be more vulnerable with my team?
Where do I need to invite God's healing for myself?

BE WILLING TO BREAK THE MOLD

When Jesus touched the man with leprosy in Matthew 8, He shattered religious expectations.

As pastors, we must prepare to break the mold:
- Turn sanctuaries into storehouses when the city is hungry.
- Open church doors as warming centers in winter.
- Show up in places your congregation doesn't expect.

During the COVID-19 crisis, we didn't just livestream services. We turned our church into a drive-through grocery distribution center. When no one else was stepping in, we offered curbside prayer. Eventually, the prayer lines stretched over a mile, and the city took notice.

It wasn't part of a five-year strategic plan. But it became part of our culture.

LEAD WITH ACTION, NOT JUST WORDS

It was Valentine's Day—one of those days when expectations and emotions run high. I hadn't made a reservation (don't judge me), so Ellen and I ended up at one of our favorite local Mexican restaurants. The only seating available was in the bar area. It wasn't ideal, but we made the most of it.

As we settled into our booth, we couldn't help but notice a man sitting alone at the bar. Twice, he slipped off his stool. His movements were heavy and sluggish—his speech slurred. It was clear he had had far too much to drink. Maybe he was heartbroken. Maybe he was numbing something far deeper than just a lonely Valentine's Day. We didn't know the backstory, but we saw the brokenness.

Others at the bar just laughed. The bartender shrugged it off. But when the man grabbed his car keys and stumbled toward the exit, I felt a knot twist in my chest.

This isn't funny. This is dangerous.

I looked at Ellen. "I think I should go out there," I said.

She nodded. "Go."

 **I DON'T KNOW WHAT WOULD HAVE HAPPENED IF I HADN'T STEPPED OUTSIDE THAT RESTAURANT.**

I stepped out into the cool night air, scanning the parking lot. There he was—already backing out of his parking spot, weaving even in reverse. He pulled forward, and within seconds, the inevitable happened.

RUN TO THE BROKENNESS

He slammed into a tree.

The front of his car crumpled like paper. My heart was pounding as I rushed toward the scene. He was trying to put the car in reverse—clearly intending to flee. I could already hear sirens in the distance. Someone else must have called 911. But right now, I was the only one on the scene.

I stepped into his path, hands up—not in judgment but in urgency.

"Sir, you can't leave. You're going to hurt someone."

His eyes were wild with fear and confusion. Nothing I said was getting through.

So, I tried something different.

"Can I pray for you?"

He froze.

The chaos in his eyes slowed for just a moment. He nodded.

I laid a hand on his shoulder and prayed aloud, asking God to bring peace, clarity, and protection. By the time the police arrived, the man had calmed enough to stay put. They took it from there.

I don't know what would have happened if I hadn't stepped outside that restaurant. But I know this: that moment reminded me that you can't build a culture of running to brokenness if you're not willing to walk toward it yourself.

It would've been easy to stay at the table and talk about how sad or dangerous the situation was. Easy to shake my head at the bartender's apathy. Easy to *say* something.

But brokenness doesn't respond to commentary—it responds to presence.

As leaders, our actions set the tone. If we want our churches to be known for engaging real pain, real risk, and real people, it has to start with us. Culture isn't crafted in vision statements or on stages. It's built in parking lots, with wrecked cars and quiet prayers.

The opportunities God gives us are often inconvenient, but they are also culture-shaping.

Culture is built when leaders choose movement over comfort.

Meet with hurting neighbors.

Walk city streets.

Listen to stories you'd rather avoid.

EXPECT FAVOR TO FOLLOW FAITHFULNESS

When we consistently show up for the broken, God often opens surprising doors.

That's why the council members who once scorned us praised us for turning our thrift store into a warming center. And that's why we were honored with the Frontline Community Hero Award.

We didn't chase influence—we chased faithfulness.

If you change the culture, you change everything.

In the next chapter, we'll explore how to mobilize your people to live out this culture so the whole church moves forward together.

APPLICATION

- Check your habits. What you do every day shapes your family, your team, and your church.
- Align your actions and values. Don't just preach outreach—live it. Don't just talk prayer—model it.
- Be willing to serve in small ways. If you can't clean toilets or stack chairs, you can't expect your people to.
- Guard your kids' culture. Parents, you are responsible for your home's culture. Yes, check the phone. Yes, set boundaries. Yes, step in.
- Shape your church's future. You can bring in the best guest speakers and run the best programs, but if the culture stays unhealthy, the church will stay stuck.

REFLECTION

1) Where are you modeling vulnerability and honesty in your leadership?
2) What brokenness in your city are you tempted to ignore?
3) Where do you need to break the mold to reach the hurting?
4) How can you invite your team and congregation into action this year?
5) Where have you seen God's favor follow faithful service, and how can you share those stories?
6) What toxic habits or behaviors need to be addressed in your life or on your team?
7) Where are you saying one thing but modeling another?

CREATING THE RIGHT CULTURE

8) What small, consistent changes can you make this month to shape a healthier culture?
9) Who in your church or home can you invite to help you cultivate a better environment?

CHAPTER 7

PASSION FOR YOUR COMMUNITY

If you don't have a passion for your community, you will limit your church's ability to become the center of it.

People can sense it. Your congregation, your city leaders, and even unchurched neighbors can feel whether you are deeply invested or if you're just passing through, looking for a better position or a more glamorous opportunity.

One of the most powerful lessons I've learned over nearly two decades of pastoring LifeBridge is this: one of the most overlooked—yet essential—ingredients to running toward brokenness is a genuine passion for the community God has placed you in. Without it, your ability—and your church's ability—to make lasting kingdom impact will be severely limited.

 YOUR LEVEL OF PASSION FOR YOUR CITY WILL SET THE CEILING FOR YOUR CHURCH'S INFLUENCE IN IT.

Lack of passion for your city does three things:

1) It limits you.

If you're constantly scanning job boards, dreaming about "greener pastures" or hoping for a new assignment, you'll miss the joy God wants to give you *right where you are*. You'll view the brokenness around you not as a divine assignment but as a burden to escape. Rather than running to it, you'll want to run from it—to another neighborhood or another church where the needs don't seem as overwhelming.

But the truth is this: every region, every city, every neighborhood has its own brokenness. Your calling is not to find the easiest place to serve—it's to be faithful wherever God has planted you: "Those who are planted in the house of the LORD shall flourish in the courts of our God" (Psalm 92:13, NKJV).

When you are rooted in your calling and passionate about your community, your spiritual bandwidth increases. You begin to see potential instead of problems. You pray differently. You lead differently. You stay long enough to make a difference.

2) It limits your church.

People in your congregation can feel when you don't truly love them or their city. They're more intuitive than you think.

If your heart is half-present, your church will reflect it. Passion leaks—or the lack of it does. And without that sense of unity and shared vision between pastor and people, trust begins to erode. And trust is the foundation of any healthy church culture.

"Then I will give you shepherds after my own heart, who will lead you with knowledge and understanding" (Jeremiah 3:15).

When you're fully invested—when your love for your community is visible and real—your people will rise to follow. They'll serve more freely. They'll trust more deeply. And they'll catch the fire of the mission God has given your church.

3) **It limits your church's ability to run to the brokenness.**

If you, as a leader, are not passionate about your community, your church won't be either. And without that passion, you will neutralize your church's ability to impact its city. The brokenness will persist, not because there's no hope but because there's no one willing to fully engage it.

Your lack of passion can become a spiritual bottleneck, stifling what God wants to do through your congregation.

"You are the light of the world. A city set on a hill cannot be hidden" (Matthew 5:14, ESV). Light doesn't run away from darkness—it shines into it. That's what the church is called to do. But we will only run toward the brokenness when we've cultivated a deep, Spirit-fueled love for the place God has called us to serve.

Your level of passion for your city will set the ceiling for your church's influence in it.

In this chapter, I want to share a few key lessons God has taught me about developing a heart for the community you're called to serve.

UNDERSTAND GOD'S HEART FOR YOUR COMMUNITY

Before you can truly love your community, you need to understand God's heart for it.

When you begin to see your city through God's eyes, everything changes:

- You stop seeing only problems, and you start seeing people.
- You stop focusing on what's wrong, and you start discerning what's possible.
- You stop measuring your city's value by its reputation, and you start measuring it by God's love for its people.

One of the prayers I pray often is: "God, break my heart for what breaks Your heart."

When we are dialed into the concerns, needs, and broken places that stir God's heart, we operate at a whole new level of favor and effectiveness. If we could somehow feel a portion of the heartbreak God feels over the brokenness of our world, it would transform everything.

Jeremiah 29:7 captures this beautifully: "Seek the peace and prosperity of the city to which I have carried you into exile. Pray to the LORD for it, because if it prospers, you too will prosper."

And remember Jesus's example in Matthew 9:36: "When he saw the crowds, he had compassion on them, because they were harassed and helpless, like sheep without a shepherd."

Our love for the community should mirror the compassion of Jesus.

BE FAITHFUL TO THE CALL GOD GAVE YOU

Here's an honest confession: Fresno, California, was never at the top of my list.

When God called my wife and me to Fresno, it wasn't because we thought it was the trendiest, most desirable place to raise a family or lead a church.

In fact, there have been seasons—hard seasons—when I hated where I lived.

And without my wife's steady, faithful heart, I might not have lasted.

There were times when I asked God, *Why here? Why not somewhere easier, somewhere more exciting, somewhere more "church-friendly"?*

There were times when I dreamed about leaving—sometimes very seriously.

But here's the thing: I've always wanted to live in the center of God's will, and I've learned that the most miserable place to be is outside of that will.

Even when my heart has wrestled, God has been faithful to hold me in place, and over time, He's given me a love for the very city I once resisted.

Psalm 37:3-4 (BSB) speaks directly to this: "Trust in the LORD and do good; dwell in the land and cultivate faithfulness. Delight yourself in the LORD, and He will give you the desires of your heart."

THE GRASS ISN'T GREENER SOMEWHERE ELSE. THE GRASS IS GREENER WHERE YOU WATER IT.

The phrase "dwell in the land" is especially powerful here. It doesn't just mean *occupy space*—it means *settle in with intention*.

It's about:

- Putting down roots in your community.
- Building real relationships across sectors—with city leaders, school officials, business owners, nonprofit directors, and neighbors.
- Cultivating a long-term vision, not a short-term mentality.

Many pastors and leaders live with what I call a "mantlepiece mindset"—they're always scanning the horizon, looking for a bigger stage, a better opportunity, or a more attractive city. But that kind of thinking robs us of joy and distracts us from the very work God has placed in front of us.

The truth is that the grass isn't greener somewhere else. The grass is greener where you water it.

When we are constantly restless, we never fully engage, and it distracts us from our calling. We miss the deep work of transformation that only comes through long-term, rooted presence.

So, pastor, I challenge you to:
- Fight the urge to keep one foot out the door.
- Resist the comparison trap.
- Dwell in the land.
- Cultivate faithfulness.
- Trust that God will bring fruit in His time.

It's been twenty years now, and I can honestly say that God has transformed my heart, even when I didn't think it was possible.

So, if you're a pastor or leader struggling to love the place where God has planted you, hear this:

Stay faithful.

Keep praying.

Ask God to break your heart open for your city.

He is faithful to reshape your affections.

YOUR PASSION WILL BE REPLICATED IN YOUR PEOPLE

This principle is simple but critical: if you're not passionate about your city, your church will be indifferent to its brokenness.

Your congregation will rarely rise above your level of engagement.

If you see your community as a stepping stone, your church will too.

If you grumble about your town, your people will too.

But if you treat your city as a mission field, your people will follow your lead.

Passion is contagious.

RUN TO THE BROKENNESS

First Corinthians 11:1 is Paul's bold invitation: "Follow my example, as I follow the example of Christ." When people see you investing in the schools, the neighborhoods, the businesses, the hurting and the marginalized, they'll be inspired to follow. When they hear you speak with hope and faith about your city, they'll catch the vision.

Over the past twenty years, we've launched plenty of initiatives at LifeBridge that were initially met with hesitation—sometimes even resistance—from trusted leaders on our team.

One of the boldest examples? Our affordable housing project.

As I've shared earlier in the book, we had the opportunity to help bring an innovative $22 million affordable housing development to our community. But when I first introduced the idea to our board and staff, let's just say . . . they thought I had lost it.

"You do realize we're pastors, right?"

"We're not real estate developers."

"This isn't what churches typically do."

They weren't wrong. We didn't have experience in housing development. We didn't have massive reserves in the bank. In fact, when I informed the board that we would need to come up with approximately $200,000 in predevelopment costs just to get the ball rolling, I could feel the tension in the room.

We all knew that kind of money wasn't sitting in our account.

But I also knew—deep in my spirit—that God was in this. So, I began to share the vision. I laid out a strategy. I talked about the kingdom impact this project could have. I reminded them of the brokenness right outside our doors—and what it would mean if our church stepped into it boldly.

AS THE PASTOR, YOU MUST CARRY THE VISION LONG BEFORE OTHERS FULLY UNDERSTAND IT.

Little by little, the team began to catch the vision.

And then something remarkable happened: One of the board members who had initially been the most hesitant—the one asking the toughest questions—approached me. He said, "I believe in this. I believe in what God is doing here. I'll front the $200,000 as a loan to get us started."

What began as hesitation became the greatest catalyst for the entire project.

This story reminds me that passion precedes progress. As the pastor, you must carry the vision long before others fully understand it. You have to burn for it, pray for it, fight for it, until the people around you begin to believe too.

Sometimes, what feels like resistance is just someone waiting to see how deeply you believe in what you're saying. And if God truly gave you the vision, your passion could help bridge the gap between skepticism and faith.

Let your passion preach, even before your plan is fully proven.

Leaders set the emotional tone. So, pastor, ministry leader, team leader:

Speak well of your city.

Invest in its flourishing.

Model a life of passion, not just a job of performance.

REFLECTIONS FROM THE JOURNEY

Looking back over the years, I can honestly say there were times when I failed at this.

There were moments when I resented where I was.

There were moments when I compared Fresno to other "destination cities" and felt jealous.

There were moments when I was tempted to retreat emotionally, even if I stayed physically.

But God's grace is bigger than our resistance. He has patiently reshaped my heart—and I've watched Him shape the heart of our church in the process.

Today, we are known as a church that loves its city. That reputation didn't come from clever branding or outreach strategies; it came from slow, steady, faithful investment. It came from saying "yes" to God's heart, even when my own heart lagged behind.

Galatians 6:9 reminds us: "Let us not become weary in doing good, for at the proper time we will reap a harvest if we do not give up."

Pastor, leader—your community needs you. Not just your sermons, not just your programs, not just your Sunday morning gatherings—it needs your heart.

If you ask God to give you His heart for your city, He will. And when He does, your people will follow—and your church will become a beacon of hope in the place where God has planted you.

So, here's the challenge:

Ask God to renew your love for your city.

Pray for eyes to see it the way He sees it.

Stop waiting for a better assignment and step into the one you already have.

Because when passion and obedience meet, miracles happen.

APPLICATION

- Pray regularly for your city. Ask God to break your heart for what breaks His.
- Stay put when you want to run. Fight the temptation to view your current assignment as a holding pattern.
- Celebrate your city's beauty and uniqueness. Even if it's not glamorous, look for the good. Speak life over your community.
- Model passion and engagement for your people. Your passion sets the tone for the entire church.

REFLECTION

1) How would you describe your current level of passion for your city?
2) What are the signs that your congregation has caught your heart for the community?
3) In what areas are you still resisting the call to love and serve your city?
4) What practical steps can you take this month to increase your engagement and passion?

CHAPTER 8

FUNDING THE MISSION

Funding local churches has never been more challenging than it is today. One of the many reasons pastors and leaders are leaving vocational ministry is that it simply doesn't pay enough to provide for their families.

When I answered the call to ministry at youth camp in 1988, I could never have imagined where that call would take me.

But today, I believe one thing with all my heart:

Your church can develop multiple streams of income that not only create an economic engine but also improve people's lives spiritually, socially, and economically, reaching people who might never set foot inside your church.

Since the beginning of the pandemic, God has taken our church on a financial journey I never could have scripted. When everything was shutting down and uncertainty was everywhere, God gave me that clear and unexpected word: "Turn your sanctuary into a storehouse."

At the time, it didn't make much sense. But we obeyed.

And because we were willing to run to the brokenness—not just spiritually but practically—we've seen God provide in miraculous ways. Since taking that step of faith, we've been able to generate just over $4.1 million in revenue, *in addition to* our regular tithes and offerings. That income has come through various social enterprises, as well as local, state, and private grants, all designed to help us meet real needs in our community.

Let me be clear: this is a flat-out miracle. But I'm convinced that the miracle didn't start with a financial strategy—it started with obedience. God honored our willingness to move toward the pain, to serve the vulnerable, and to reimagine how the church can meet practical needs.

In this chapter, I want to show you how your church, no matter its size or resources, can begin to develop additional income streams to fund the mission God has given you. These are not gimmicks. They're gospel-driven, community-centered, and mission-aligned opportunities that can help your church become sustainable, scalable, and more deeply embedded in the life of your city.

THE DECLINE IN CHURCH GIVING

Recent data underscores the urgency of this issue:
- ▸ Only 5 percent of churchgoers tithe regularly, and half of those who donate give about 2 percent of their income.
- ▸ Giving to religious organizations has declined from 63 percent of total charitable giving in 1983 to just 24 percent in 2023.

FUNDING THE MISSION

> Average giving by adults at US Protestant churches is about $17 a week.[11]

The decline in church giving is a multifaceted issue influenced by various economic, theological, and demographic factors. Here's an in-depth look at the primary reasons:

1) Economic Uncertainty. Economic instability, including inflation and job insecurity, has significantly impacted individuals' ability to contribute financially to churches. A report from Vox highlights that fewer than half of American households now give cash to charity, attributing this decline to factors like rising living costs and economic strain.[12]

2) Theological Shifts and Debates on Tithing. There's a growing trend of theological perspectives that question the traditional practice of tithing. According to Barna Research, only 21 percent of Christians set their church giving at 10 percent or more of their income, with 25 percent not giving to their church at all. This shift in belief systems affects consistent financial support for churches.[13]

3) Socioeconomic Challenges in Certain Communities. Churches located in lower socioeconomic areas often face greater challenges in securing financial contributions The average churchgoer gives less than 3 percent of their income to the church, which can be particularly

---

[11] Church Trac, "The State of Church Giving: Trends and Statistics [2025]," *Churchtrac Blog*, https://www.churchtrac.com/articles/the-state-of-church-giving?
[12] Celia Ford, "Are we actually in the middle of a generosity crisis?", *Vox*, 20 Nov. 2024, https://www.vox.com/future-perfect/359526/charitable-giving-generosity-crisis-report-americans-young?.
[13] Wikipedia, "Decline of Christianity in the Western world," last updated 2 Jun. 2025, https://en.wikipedia.org/wiki/Decline_of_Christianity_in_the_Western_world?.

limiting for congregations in economically disadvantaged regions.[14]

4) New Converts and the Journey to Generosity. New believers may take time to understand and embrace the practice of regular giving. Statistics show that only about 5 percent of churchgoers tithe, indicating that many congregants, especially new ones, may not immediately contribute financially at expected levels.[15]

5) Declining Church Attendance. A significant decrease in church attendance correlates with reduced giving. It's estimated that 40 million adults (16 percent of American adults) have stopped attending church over the past twenty-five years, reshaping the landscape of philanthropy and affecting church donations.[16]

These factors collectively contribute to the decline in church giving. Addressing them requires a multifaceted approach, including financial education, theological discussions on generosity, community engagement, and strategies to reconnect with lapsed attendees.

These trends highlight the need for churches to explore alternative funding avenues to sustain and expand their ministries.

---

[14] Tithe.ly, "10 Key Trends and Statistics for Church Donations," 12 Oct. 2024, https://get.tithe.ly/blog/10-key-trends-and-statistics-for-church-donations?.
[15] Tithe.ly, "10 Key Trends."
[16] Jeremy Reis, "Fundraising Trend: Decline in Church Attendance Affecting Giving," *NonProfit Fundraising*, 2 Dec. 2024, https://nonprofitfundraising.com/fundraising-trend-decline-in-church-attendance-affecting-giving/?.

MULTIPLE STREAMS OF INCOME

In early 2020, we had three employees. By the end of the year, we had over forty. Prior to the pandemic, we had one stream of income, and by the end of the pandemic, we had six streams of income.

 **WE DIDN'T INVENT THE NEED— WE SIMPLY DISCOVERED IT.**

The pandemic, as devastating as it was, forced us to pivot, not just for survival but for kingdom innovation. Suddenly, the traditional ways of doing church weren't enough. Our community had needs like never before, and we began to ask a simple but dangerous question:

What if God wants to birth something new out of this crisis?

So, we prayed. We listened. We paid attention. We started talking to our neighbors, school principals, city leaders, single moms, unemployed fathers, and overlooked teenagers. We didn't invent the need—we simply discovered it.

That shift led us to:

> **Launch a preschool** because local families told us they couldn't find safe, affordable childcare, and we had the space and the people to do something about it.

> **Start a separate nonprofit** because we began receiving more calls from city agencies, foundations, and school

districts wanting to partner with us but needed to do so through a separate legal and funding structure.
- **Open a thrift store** because we were already giving away clothes, but people wanted a dignified, consistent, and affordable place to shop. That store met real needs *and* created jobs.
- **Open an event center** because we needed sustainable income to support ministry. A friend from our church had the industry expertise and vision to help us launch. That dream grew beyond anything we could have imagined. God opened a door for us to **lease an incredible event center property** despite competing bids from national chains. When I asked the owner of the property (who wasn't even a Christ follower) why he chose us over multimillion-dollar companies, he shrugged and said: *"I don't know.... I guess God told me to lease it to you."* Which reminds me, if God is in it, nothing can stop what God is birthing.
- **We also launched a Spanish-speaking campus (although not technically a social enterprise)** because so many families in our neighborhood speak Spanish as their first language, and we wanted them to hear the gospel in their heart language.

None of these things came out of thin air. They were birthed in prayer, tested through relationship, confirmed by community feedback, and fueled by obedience.

We didn't sit in a boardroom and dream up ideas. We got out into the streets and asked, "Where's the brokenness? And what can we do about it?"

God took our yes and did the rest.

WHAT IS A SOCIAL ENTERPRISE?

A social enterprise is an organization that applies commercial strategies to maximize financial, social, and environmental well-being.

In practical terms for churches:
- It's another income stream that helps fund ministry.
- It's a way to create jobs and opportunities for people in your congregation and community.
- It's a tool to reach people spiritually who might never come to a Sunday service.

Starting a social enterprise isn't just a good idea—it's a strategic way to live out the gospel in action. Here's why it could be the right next step for your church.

It helps fund the church's work. Depending solely on tithes and offerings is becoming increasingly difficult. Even though we will always teach biblical generosity, as noted, statistics show tithing rates are declining year after year.

For us, the pandemic not only changed how we did ministry, it radically multiplied our monthly income through social enterprises. We've seen a near-quadrupling of revenue, allowing us to expand ministry and hire staff.

It provides jobs for the unemployed and underemployed. One of the best ways to disciple people is by helping them learn the value of work.

Remember Jonathan, the high-functioning special needs adult who had never held a job? The day he received his first paycheck from our thrift store, he cried, and now he faithfully serves on our usher team.

Nathan and Alexis, both young parents, shared how employment at our event center provided the stability they needed to care for their families and pay their rent.

It creates a competitive advantage. The people in your congregation represent a vast relational network. When you launch a social enterprise, you automatically have a marketing and referral engine built in, far beyond what most small businesses could access.

More importantly, people in your city will often choose to support a nonprofit social enterprise over a national chain, especially when they know their dollars are staying local and making a difference.

It places your church in the marketplace. Our social enterprises have given us an entirely new mission field: people who would never come to a church service.

One of the most unexpected blessings of launching a social enterprise is seeing how it becomes a tool not just for funding ministry but for transforming lives.

 **IT'S NOT JUST ABOUT REVENUE. IT'S ABOUT REDEMPTION.**

Take Luis, for example.

Luis is now our sales manager at the event center we operate, but that's not how his story began. He didn't start coming to our church because of a sermon or invitation. He came because we hired him.

At the time, Luis was just looking for a job. He had been battling alcoholism and wasn't connected to any church. When we posted the position on Indeed, he applied, not because he was looking for ministry but because something about a church owning and operating an event center intrigued him. In his words, "It was compelling. I'd never seen a church do something like this."

That simple job posting turned into something far greater.

As he worked with us, he experienced the culture of our team, the presence of God in our daily operations, and the way we live out our mission, even in the business side of things. This past Good Friday, Luis rededicated his life to Christ during service. He's now walking in freedom from addiction, and his life has taken a completely new direction.

Would that have happened if we hadn't launched the event center? Maybe not.

That's the beauty of social enterprise. It funds the mission and becomes the mission. It creates spaces where people like Luis encounter God in ways they never expected—through a job, through a relationship, through a purpose-filled business. When your church steps into the marketplace with intentionality, it's not just about revenue. It's about redemption of people who first encounter us through our event center, thrift store, or preschool, and later walk through the doors of our sanctuary.

Marketplace ministry opens new doors for evangelism, discipleship, and influence.

HOW TO START A SOCIAL ENTERPRISE IN YOUR CHURCH

As you've read, developing multiple streams of income is not just a smart financial move; it's a kingdom opportunity. But how do you actually get started? Here's a practical roadmap to help you take the first steps:

1) **Find a Need in Your Community—and Fill It.**

Start with prayer and observation. What gap exists in your community that your church could fill?

- Are there not enough affordable preschools?
- Is there a shortage of event venues?
- Is there a need for job training, thrift stores, affordable housing, food distribution, or counseling services?

Ask God to help you see the brokenness that's waiting for a solution. As you discern the need, begin exploring what it would take to fill that gap. John asks in 1 John 3:17 (ESV): "But if anyone has the world's goods and sees his brother in need, yet closes his heart against him, how does God's love abide in him?"

2) **Leverage the Relational Equity in Your Church.**

God has already placed people in your congregation who carry passion, experience, or gifting in the areas you're considering.

- Who has experience in business, hospitality, childcare, education, retail, real estate, finance, or nonprofit work?
- Who has a passion for helping others, mentoring, or creating job opportunities?

3) **You don't have to know everything yourself—you just need to gather the right team.**

Proverbs 15:22 says, "Plans fail for lack of counsel, but with many advisers they succeed."

4) **Tap Into People's Passion.**
People will help build what they believe in.
- Share the vision from the platform and in smaller meetings.
- Tell stories
- Ask people to pray, volunteer, and offer their expertise.

This is how momentum builds and how buy-in deepens.

5) **Start Small, Build Incrementally.**
You don't need to launch a massive enterprise overnight. Start small, test your idea, learn as you go.

For example:
- We originally launched our event center with the modest goal of hosting forty events per year—but today, we're booking over 150 annually across two venues. For the past two years, it's even been nominated "Best of the Central Valley." I'm still in awe of what God has done!
- We started our preschool to meet a need in the neighborhood, and one of the most sought-after programs in the community.

Small steps lead to significant impact.

6) **Consider Creating a Separate Nonprofit.**
Starting a nonprofit can:
- Expand your reach beyond Sunday morning.
- Open up grant funding and community partnerships unavailable to churches.
- Give you credibility and favor in the secular marketplace.
- Allow you to partner with government agencies, businesses, and other nonprofits.

We've been able to secure grants, launch projects, and impact thousands of people precisely because we established a separate nonprofit arm alongside our church.

7) **Learn from Others—You're Not Alone.**

Look for case studies, visit churches doing this well, and reach out for advice.

If we can do it, so can you. To date, since the beginning of the pandemic, we've raised over $4,100,000 outside of our general tithe and offerings for kingdom work through social enterprises and grants, and I believe God can multiply this in your ministry too.

8) **Leverage the Holy Spirit.**

Every social enterprise we've launched since the beginning of the pandemic, from our thrift store to the preschool to the event center and now serving as a distribution hub, didn't begin with a business plan.

It began with a whisper.

It was the power of the Holy Spirit that gave us the ingenuity, the insight, and the favor to start things we never would've dreamed up on our own. The creativity didn't come just from a whiteboard session; it also came from time in God's presence.

First Corinthians 2:10-11 reminds us: "These are the things God has revealed to us by his Spirit. The Spirit searches all things, even the deep things of God." When we lean into the Spirit, we're tapping into divine creativity. God reveals things—needs we couldn't see, strategies we wouldn't think of, doors we didn't know could open.

FUNDING THE MISSION

The early church relied on this. It was the Holy Spirit who told Philip to approach the Ethiopian eunuch (Acts 8). It was the Holy Spirit who set apart Paul and Barnabas for mission (Acts 13). It was the Holy Spirit who gave wisdom to Stephen, power to Peter, and strategy to the apostles.

We must depend on that same Spirit today.

It's not just prayer that launches ministry—it's Spirit-empowered prayer that positions us for innovation.

Before you start brainstorming your next outreach or social enterprise, ask:

Holy Spirit, what are You already doing in my city?

Where are You inviting us to join You?

What brokenness have You already given us favor to step into?

Zechariah 4:6 says it best: "Not by might nor by power, but by My Spirit." That includes grant applications, facility decisions, budgets, staffing, zoning approvals—every step of launching and sustaining mission-driven enterprises.

God's vision requires God's power. Don't just lean on a good idea. Lean on the Holy Spirit, and you'll see favor flow in ways that only heaven could orchestrate.

Pastor, this is not just about money. It's about mission. You are called to transform lives, families, and neighborhoods, and funding the mission is part of that call.

Psalm 112:5 reminds us that "Good will come to those who are generous and lend freely, who conduct their affairs with justice."

Let's believe God for bold ideas, creative strategies, and supernatural provision for the sake of the gospel and the flourishing of your community.

APPLICATION
- Keep your heart aligned with God's heart.
- Keep your mission clear.
- Remember: this is about expanding your reach, not just padding your budget.

REFLECTION
1) **What current needs exist in your community that your church could help meet through a social enterprise?** Think practically—childcare, job training, food insecurity, or affordable housing. What gap is your church uniquely positioned to fill?
2) **How might creating multiple income streams strengthen, not distract from, your church's mission?** Reflect on how financial sustainability can support both spiritual and practical ministry.
3) **Do you currently have people in your congregation with business, nonprofit, or community experience?** What would it look like to invite them into the vision of a church-run enterprise?
4) **How do you view money in ministry—primarily as a necessity or as a tool for transformation?** Examine how your theology of stewardship impacts your willingness to pursue creative funding models.
5) **What's one small step you could take in the next ninety days toward launching or exploring a social enterprise?** It could be a meeting, a community conversation, or even writing a vision statement.

CHAPTER 9

OCCUPATIONAL HAZARDS OF MINISTRY

When we think of high-risk jobs, one that immediately comes to mind is a high-voltage power line technician, also known as a lineman. These men and women climb poles and towers, often hundreds of feet in the air, to maintain and repair electrical lines carrying tens of thousands of volts. One wrong move can result in death. The job requires intense focus, thick protective gear, and ongoing training. It's dangerous—and everyone knows it.

Because the danger is so obvious, linemen don't approach their work casually. They respect the risk, prepare meticulously, and stay tethered to the safety systems that protect their lives. Their routines are shaped by the awareness that they're always one slip away from disaster.

Now, compare that to pastoral ministry.

No one hands you a hard hat or safety harness when you become a pastor. You don't feel a jolt of electricity when someone gossips behind your back or when you're blindsided by a leadership betrayal. But make no mistake—ministry has its own high-voltage danger. Only it's not your body that's most at risk; it's your soul and, even more alarming, your family's soul.

 **MANY PASTORS DON'T REALIZE THE DANGER UNTIL IT'S TOO LATE.**

Where the lineman may suffer a physical fall, the ministry leader often suffers an emotional or spiritual one. Burnout, bitterness, isolation, and depression are all too common. And unlike linemen, many pastors don't realize the danger until it's too late because it's silent, slow, and invisible.

Here's a critical warning:
- Median worship attendance in US churches dropped from 137 to sixty-five over two decades.[17]
- In 2019, 4,500 churches closed while only 3,000 were planted.[18]

Much of this decline is due to unresolved internal conflict.

That's why this chapter matters. If we don't recognize and prepare for the emotional and spiritual hazards of ministry, we'll become another casualty in the field. But with God's help, intentional rhythms, and a supportive community, we can not only survive the risk—we can thrive in the calling.

---

[17] Yonat Shimron, "Study: Attendance Hemorrhaging at Small and Midsize US Congregations," *Church Leaders*, 15 Oct. 2021, https://churchleaders.com/news/407585-congregational-attendance.html?.
[18] Yonat Shimron, "Study: More Churches Closing than Opening," *Ministry Watch*, 27 May 2021, https://ministrywatch.com/study-more-churches-closing-than-opening/?.

OCCUPATIONAL HAZARDS OF MINISTRY

Although this subject is rarely talked about, it's critical to face it head-on. There are at least four key occupational hazards in ministry we must recognize and confront:

1) Becoming a Casualty of Others' Brokenness

This is one of the most difficult occupational hazards in ministry. Turns out that when you and your church run to the brokenness, you will encounter broken people, and that comes at a cost. Ministry often means being wounded by the very people you're trying to help, and sometimes, those are the deepest wounds you'll ever incur in ministry—those from within the church, not outside of it.

Jesus said in Luke 17:1 (NKJV): "It is impossible that no offenses should come."

If you've been in ministry for even a few weeks, you've likely already experienced this. There's a unique pain when someone you have poured into wounds you. It's one of the hardest hazards to prepare for. I experienced this firsthand in a way that nearly broke me.

In 2020, I received a clear and compelling word from the Lord. It wasn't just a nice thought or a personal goal—it was a holy conviction. God spoke to me and said, "The ACTS Foundation will make a significant impact on poverty in our city."

I believed Him with everything in me. I didn't just believe, I ran. I moved with urgency and obedience. And soon, the vision started coming to life. As I mentioned earlier, we were given an opportunity to lead a $22 million affordable housing project in Fresno. This wasn't just a sketch on a whiteboard—it was a real plan with a real team and real momentum.

I could see the future so clearly: families in safe, affordable homes. Parents no longer forced to choose between rent and groceries. A place of hope and stability for youth aging out of foster care. The forgotten corners of our city becoming centers of opportunity.

But then, everything unraveled. The reason why we don't own and operate the housing project today is a casualty of others' brokenness.

Two people who were close to me, both deeply disgruntled, made false accusations to the Fresno City Council. Politics got involved. People who didn't know us and didn't care about the truth jumped in. Leaders in our own city—the very place we had sacrificed so much to serve—voted to reject our project.

I was devastated.

It felt like a holy dream had been buried. The grief was real. I mourned that loss like you mourn a death. And I found myself asking, *God, why did You allow this? We were doing what You called us to do.*

However, God does not waste broken dreams.

 **WHAT'S BURIED TODAY CAN RISE TOMORROW.**

In the two years that followed, when it felt like all was lost, we did not give up. We didn't get bitter. We got to work. We prayed. We trained. We built in secret. And behind the scenes, we prepared to become a provider of CalAIM, social services funded by the state of California, an initiative that would allow us to walk alongside some of the most vulnerable people in our city with real, holistic care.

And now, as I write this, we've launched.

We are serving hundreds of individuals and families, not just with groceries but with case management, healthcare navigation, and the kind of wraparound support that changes lives.

And here's what's incredible: through CalAIM, our impact on poverty will surpass what we could have accomplished through that housing project.

Yes, the dream died. But it was not the end. Like a seed planted in the ground, it was buried only to bring forth something even greater.

This is the cost of running to the brokenness. This is the cost of being a shepherd in the trenches. Sometimes, people bite the very hand that's trying to feed them. Sometimes, people attack what they don't understand. But if you stay faithful, if you keep going, God will resurrect what was buried and multiply it (Galatians 6:9).

Ministry can make you a casualty, but it can also make you a conduit for restoration. What's buried today can rise tomorrow. Stay faithful. Your dream may be in the ground, but it's not gone. It's just waiting to grow.

So, how can we withstand these wounds?

- Pray and release them to God. Take your hurt to Him before it hardens.
- Avoid pushing people's buttons. As Paul says in Romans 12:18, "If it is possible, as far as it depends on you, live at peace with everyone."

> **Understand the sovereignty of God.** Looking back on that season, I'm now deeply thankful that we are not the ones operating the housing project. With time and perspective, I can clearly see how God used me, our church, and our nonprofit to help bring this innovative initiative to our community, but His intention was for us to help birth it and then pass it on. Another incredible nonprofit in our city has taken the baton and carried it forward with excellence. And as of this writing, they're just two weeks away from the ribbon-cutting ceremony—a moment they've graciously invited me to attend.

Furthermore, I've learned something profound through it all: when God calls you to do something significant, you may or may not experience the full fruit of that work, and that's okay. God calls some people to plant, others to water, and others still to harvest (1 Corinthians 3:6-7). The outcome isn't up to us; it's up to Him. When we learn to rest in His sovereignty, we're freed from striving, from comparison, and from disappointment. And that peace allows us to thrive right where He's placed us.

Ask yourself:

Are you rehearsing old wounds?

Are you losing hope because of what someone did to you?

If so, it may be time to walk the hard road of forgiveness and not allow the brokenness of others to derail your calling or your mission.

Remember the story I shared earlier about Martin and Mary, the couple who caused significant division in our church? Their actions didn't just hurt my feelings. They hurt people. They fractured trust. They led a campaign that resulted in a 35 percent loss of our church's revenue and nearly 40 percent of our attendance. Because of that financial impact, I had to take a pay cut, and we lost the first home we had ever purchased in California.

So, when God began challenging me to truly forgive them, I struggled. I wrestled with it. How do you forgive someone who has cost you so much?

Then, about two years ago, I attended a pastor's conference in our city. It was during a worship set; the room was full, the music was loud, and my hands were lifted high in surrender to God. Out of nowhere, I felt a hand grab my arm.

It was Martin.

He had tears in his eyes and simply said, "Pastor Kevin, I need to ask for your forgiveness. I was wrong. I gossiped. I tried to destroy what God was building. And I'm so sorry."

In that holy moment, God gave me the strength I didn't have on my own. I looked him in the eye and said, "Martin, you really hurt me. You hurt our church. We lost our house because of what happened. But yes—I forgive you."

He broke down sobbing and hugged me. It was one of the most healing moments of my ministry.

Forgiveness doesn't excuse what happened, but it frees you from carrying the weight of it. And sometimes, the freedom you offer others becomes the freedom you didn't know you needed.

2) **Leading Through the Tension of Frustration**

Frustration is the occupational hazard nobody talks about. Ministry frustration comes from the gap between what we expect and what we experience. We live in the tension between the "world that is"—the messy, broken, not-yet-what-we-hoped version of reality—and the "world that could be"—the vision that God has placed on our hearts. This is where frustration lives, and this dissonance can exhaust even the most faithful leader.

Not all frustration is bad. In fact, some frustration can be holy. There are two types of frustration in ministry: generative and destructive.

> - Generative frustration is a holy discontent that fuels your passion. It's what I like to call the "Popeye moment"—that inner stirring that says, "That's all I can stands; I can't stands no more." It pushes you to act, to lead, to build.
> - Destructive frustration, on the other hand, is a fleshly discontent that drains your passion and joy. It's the slow erosion of your calling under the weight of disappointment, unmet expectations, and burnout.

Frustration is the occupational hazard of ministry. A construction worker might drive a nail through their hand. Our wounds are often unseen but just as real.

Paul expresses his own struggle with his frustration in Galatians 4:18-20 (MSG):

It is a good thing to be passionate in doing good, but not just when I am in your presence. Can't you continue the same concern for both my person and my message when I am away from you that you had when I was with you? Do you know how I feel right now, and will feel until Christ's life becomes visible in your lives? Like a mother in the pain of childbirth. Oh, I keep wishing that I was with you. Then

OCCUPATIONAL HAZARDS OF MINISTRY

I wouldn't be reduced to this blunt, letter-writing language out of sheer frustration.

You can feel the ache in Paul's words. His frustration wasn't because people stopped showing up to church. It was deeper than that—they had grown cold in their passion for the gospel. He loved them deeply, but their spiritual inconsistency pained him.

This is ministry—walking the tightrope of deep compassion for people while being thoroughly frustrated by their lack of commitment.

When I launched LifeBridge, I was warned about this. Veteran pastors told me one of the biggest reasons church plants fail is not due to lack of gifting or vision but the dissonance between expectations and reality.

I poured my heart into sermons, only to see a room half empty. I rallied teams and cast vision, only to face burnout and apathy. Like Paul, I wondered, "Has all my hard work gone up in smoke?" (Galatians 4:11, author paraphrase)

Frustration doesn't always show up as tears or anger. Sometimes, it's more subtle but just as dangerous. Here are three signs you're experiencing ministry frustration:

- You're short and snappy with those closest to you. Your family gets the brunt of your internal stress.
- You're highly critical. You begin criticizing yourself, your staff, your spouse, and even the people you're called to shepherd.
- Your tone shifts in your preaching. During a recent vacation, I visited a church where the pastor clearly loved God, but his tone toward the congregation was

condescending. I could sense his frustration in every word. That's a warning sign.

You may feel like quitting, but the call remains. You still have to preach, lead, encourage, parent, and shepherd through it all. Here's how:

- Admit your frustration. We often hide it because we feel like we're letting God down. Our spirits say, God is with you, but our flesh screams, You're done!
- Admitting your frustration to God is not weakness—it's worship. Paul modeled this vulnerability: "Do you know how I feel right now?" (Galatians 4:20, MSG) Whether you're an extrovert who shares with trusted friends or an introvert who journals in solitude, bring your frustration into the light. You'll feel lighter.
- Remember, your identity isn't tied to results. Your value isn't based on how many people show up or whether you met the budget this month. Psalm 46:1-2 reminds us: "God is our refuge and strength, an ever-present help in trouble. Therefore we will not fear, though the earth give way and the mountains fall into the heart of the sea." Your worth is rooted in your calling, not your current numbers.
- Focus on the vision. God gave you a picture of what your church could become. Keep your eyes on that vision.
- Remember the call. When was the moment God called you? Go back there in your mind. Rehearse it in your heart. That calling is what sustains you in the valley.
- Trust God's sovereignty. First Corinthians 3:7 reminds us: "So neither the one who plants nor the one who waters is

anything, but only God, who makes things grow." You can rest in the truth that God—not you—provides the increase.
- Celebrate the small wins. Every time you feed someone who is hungry, every salvaged marriage, every new believer, every child in your kids' ministry is a victory worth celebrating. These moments matter more than metrics. If you pastor in one place long enough, you are very well aware that there are seasons of momentum and seasons when you feel stuck. In the seasons when you feel stuck, celebrating what may seem like small wins is so crucial in overcoming ministry frustration.
- Frustration will come. But God is faithful. If He can part the sea, move mountains, and feed multitudes, He can also breathe new passion into your weary soul. He can empower you to lead through the occupational hazards of ministry—and come out stronger on the other side.

3) Comparing Yourself to Other Churches

In today's social media age, pastors fall into the sin of comparing themselves to churches across the world with a swipe of the thumb. But 2 Corinthians 10:12 (NKJV) warns us: "But they, measuring themselves by themselves, and comparing themselves among themselves, are not wise."

Comparison can strangle the joy out of ministry. Remember:
- Your calling is unique. No one is quite like you, and that's by design!
- Your context is unique.
- Your pace is unique.

If you find yourself endlessly measuring against others, pause and realign your heart.

4) **Insecurity**

Ministry work is unusually public, and with that public visibility comes vulnerability. Failure feels amplified; success can feel fleeting.

OVERCOMING INSECURITY IN MINISTRY: THE STORY OF MOSES

Insecurity is one of the most silent yet destructive occupational hazards of ministry. It creeps in quietly but can sabotage a leader's calling, confidence, and capacity to run toward the brokenness. One of the most powerful biblical examples of insecurity in leadership comes from the life of Moses.

In Exodus 4:10, we find Moses standing on holy ground, receiving a divine assignment that would alter history. God had just revealed His plan to deliver the Israelites from the oppression of Egypt, and Moses was His chosen leader. The assignment was clear. The plan was laid out. Miracles had been demonstrated before his eyes. Yet Moses doubted.

Rather than embracing his call, Moses debated with God: "O Lord, I'm not very good with words. I never have been, and I'm not now, even though you have spoken to me. I get tongue-tied, and my words get tangled" (Exodus 4:10, NLT).

Even after God performed two miracles (turning his staff into a snake and back and then healing his hand from leprosy), Moses still couldn't see how God could use him. He believed in his weakness more than he believed in God's strength.

God's response wasn't one of condemnation but of reassurance: "Who makes a person's mouth? Who decides whether people speak or do not speak. . . . Is it not I, the LORD? Now go! I will be with you as you speak, and I will instruct you in what to say" (Exodus 4:11-12, NLT).

Still, Moses resisted. He begged God to send someone else. And while God still used Moses powerfully, Moses missed out on the fullness of what God originally intended, so he had to rely on Aaron as his spokesperson.

I've often wrestled with insecurity at different points throughout my ministry. Like Moses, I've questioned whether I was truly the right person for the job. As a child, I struggled significantly with stuttering. In fact, I was placed in special education classes because of it. I never imagined that one day, I'd be standing in front of people, proclaiming God's Word. But that's the incredible humor—and favor—of God. He delights in using the most unlikely people to accomplish His purposes. Every time insecurity creeps in, I go back to my calling. I remember that God didn't call me because I was the most polished or articulate; He called me because He saw something in me I couldn't yet see in myself. And that reminder helps me move forward with courage.

 **YOU DON'T HAVE TO WAIT UNTIL YOU FEEL "READY." IN CHRIST, YOU ALREADY ARE.**

Moses didn't feel like enough, and he let that insecurity shape his response. But what if he had trusted God's call from the start? What if he had believed that God's presence was enough to make him enough? That's the invitation for you too.

Here's why you're enough:

1) You're Called by Christ

Like Moses, many pastors and leaders feel overwhelmed and question whether they're the right person for the job. But if God has called you, He will equip you.

"In his kindness God called you to his eternal glory by means of Jesus Christ" (1 Peter 5:10, NLT).

"You are a chosen people... God's very own possession... you can show others the goodness of God, for he called you out of the darkness into his wonderful light" (1 Peter 2:9, NLT).

You don't have to strive for validation. You are called, and that calling is your foundation.

2) You're Capable Through Christ

Moses had an insecurity problem. He believed in his weakness more than he believed in God's power. And we do the same. We let insecurity speak louder than our calling.

"I can do all things through [Christ] who gives me strength" (Philippians 4:13).

"We are more than conquerors through him who loved us" (Romans 8:37).

"Not that we are competent in ourselves... but our competence comes from God" (2 Corinthians 3:4-5).

Christ's strength is made perfect in our weakness. You are more capable than you realize because your capability comes from Christ.

3) You're Complete in Christ

Even when we feel unfinished or unqualified, God says we're already complete through Christ.

"His divine power has given us everything we need for a godly life" (2 Peter 1:3).

"For in Christ all the fullness of God lives in a human body, so you are also complete through your union with Christ" (Colossians 2:9-10, NLT).

You don't have to wait until you feel "ready." In Christ, you already are.

THE COST OF INSECURITY

In the end, Moses couldn't believe God would use him, even with all the evidence. So, God allowed Aaron to be his mouthpiece. Moses still led the people out of Egypt, but he missed God's best by not fully trusting God's choice.

Let me ask you a question:

Could you be missing out on God's best for your ministry because you feel like you're not enough?

The presence of God speaks clearly. You are enough, not because of your resume, not because of your eloquence, but because Christ is in you.

Pastor, you're called. You're capable. You're complete.

And if God could use a tongue-tied shepherd to deliver a nation, He can use you to lead your church, serve your community, and run to the brokenness.

Believe again. Trust again. And go forward—in His strength.

If you are weighed down by unresolved hurt, frustration, comparison, or insecurity, you will struggle to run to the brokenness in your community. As pastors, we all carry some level of brokenness, but we must avoid major wounds that can derail the mission.

I strongly encourage you to ask for help if you have experienced one of these silent but potentially ministry-killing occupational hazards. You must address your own brokenness to run to the brokenness. You are too valuable to burn out quietly. God called you, He will sustain you, and He has placed you where you are for a reason.

If God can do the impossible—and He can—He can empower you to endure and overcome the hazards of ministry.

APPLICATION

- Assess your heart: Where are you carrying offense, frustration, or insecurity?
- Adopt a conflict resolution model: Teach your leaders how you will handle issues.
- Admit when you need help: Reach out to trusted mentors, counselors, or even to me if you have no one else.
- Protect your joy: You cannot lead others to healing if you are spiritually hemorrhaging.
- Lean into the Holy Spirit: Remember, you have the Spirit that hovered over creation (Genesis 1) inside you. You are called to lead with supernatural creativity and resilience.

REFLECTION

1) **How have you experienced the pain of others' brokenness in your ministry?** Are there relationships that have left you wounded or discouraged? What steps can you take to begin healing and forgiveness?

2) **What kind of frustration are you currently experiencing—generative or destructive?** How is it affecting your leadership, preaching, or relationships? What rhythms or supports do you need to stay grounded and refreshed?

3) **Do you find yourself comparing your ministry to others?** What triggers that comparison? How can you practically shift your mindset to celebrate your unique calling and context?

4) **Where does insecurity creep into your leadership?** What lies are you tempted to believe about your adequacy or value? How can you renew your confidence in God's call, equipping, and presence in your life?

5) **What practices help you stay emotionally and spiritually healthy in ministry?** Do you have a mentor, counselor, or trusted friend to talk to? Are there warning signs in your life that it's time to pause and get help?

6) **How can you create a culture on your team that prioritizes emotional health and vulnerability?** What conversations might need to happen? How can you model honesty, humility, and hope?

7) **What small win can you celebrate today?** Take time to thank God for one moment of impact, one changed life, or one answered prayer. How can you make celebration a regular rhythm for yourself and your team?

8) **Are you trusting God's sovereignty with your ministry outcomes?** In what areas do you need to release control? How would embracing God's timing and process bring peace to your leadership?

CHAPTER 10

YOU CAN CHANGE YOUR COMMUNITY

I consider myself an average guy—an "average Joe"—who sometimes wonders why God would choose to use someone like me. Surely, I've thought, He could find someone more gifted, more charismatic, or more polished. But here's the truth: God isn't looking for perfect resumes—He's looking for willing hearts.

All God requires is your availability, your surrender, and your passion to be used by Him. That's when the extraordinary begins to flow through ordinary people and churches.

I'll never forget when God called me to ministry. I was at an Illinois youth camp when Gary Zelesky gave an altar call, saying, "If you feel called to full-time ministry, don't walk to the altar—run!"

And I did. I ran down that aisle, sobbing, completely overwhelmed by the presence of God.

RUN TO THE BROKENNESS

Whenever I go through hard times in ministry—when I feel like giving up or question if I'm making a difference—I go back to that moment. That calling has carried me through ups and downs, disappointments and breakthroughs, heartbreaks and celebrations.

Where did God call you? Go back there in your heart. Remembering your first calling will help you finish your calling. When we stay rooted in that original calling, God often expands our influence beyond what we imagined.

One of the greatest joys in ministry for me has not only been seeing the impact increase at LifeBridge but also watching how we've been able to multiply that impact by helping other local churches. Through partnerships like the one we have with Convoy of Hope, we now resource twenty-five local churches and nonprofits with food and supplies, equipping them to run to the brokenness in their own neighborhoods. To me, that's even more fulfilling than what we can accomplish as a single congregation.

Just last month, we distributed over 100,000 pounds of food to these churches. Why? Because we believe a scared world needs a fearless church.

As Paul encourages in 2 Timothy 4:7: "I have fought the good fight, I have finished the race, I have kept the faith." That's what we want to be able to say when we stand before Jesus one day, when we hear, "Well *done*, good and faithful servant.... Enter into the joy of your lord" (Matthew 25:23, NKJV).

But finishing the race and keeping the faith doesn't happen by default—it requires confronting the fears that quietly undermine our calling. Too often, pastors and leaders operate from this fear—fear of failure, fear of scarcity, fear of rejection, or fear of "What if it doesn't work?" But I'm convinced the enemy of our souls works hard to keep us from stepping out, trying new things, and trusting God to use us to impact our communities. We must break agreement with fear and choose faith. That choice begins with believing two simple—but powerful—truths.

1) God Uses Average People and Churches to Do Extraordinary Things.

You have read about the miracles God has done for us in this book—there is no reason that God is unable to do the same for you.

When others saw a shepherd boy, God saw a king.

In 1 Samuel 16, when the prophet Samuel came to anoint the next king of Israel, everyone assumed it would be one of Jesse's older, stronger sons. But God told Samuel, "Do not consider his appearance or his height. . . . The LORD does not look at the things people look at. People look at the outward appearance, but the LORD looks at the heart" (1 Samuel 16:7).

And so, the youngest, the overlooked one, the shepherd in the fields—David—was chosen and anointed king.

This story is a powerful reminder that you don't need to have the biggest building, the flashiest worship team, or the most Instagram followers for God to use you. What matters is knowing God and being available for His purposes. As Daniel 11:32 (NKJV) says, "But the people who know their God shall be strong, and carry out *great exploits*."

The only qualification that matters? Knowing your God.

2) **Commit Wholeheartedly to Becoming a Church That Runs to the Brokenness.**
Don't dabble in outreach—dive in.
Don't tiptoe around brokenness—run to it.

When you commit to this with your whole heart, you'll begin to see favor, opportunities, and influence multiply in ways you could never have manufactured in your own strength.

Here's a practical roadmap to start:

- Identify the biggest needs in your community. We went from picking up stray shopping carts along Shaw Avenue to helping bring one of Fresno's most innovative affordable housing projects to life. That journey started with simply identifying a need. When you begin meeting needs, God opens doors of favor and influence.
- Do something today to run toward the brokenness. Don't overthink it. Take one step today, whether it's starting a food pantry, offering free tutoring, opening your building to community groups, or visiting with local officials to learn their greatest concerns.
- Become a "run to the brokenness" church. Make it part of your culture, your language, and your DNA.

At the beginning of this book, I shared the simple but audacious dream Ellen and I had when we moved to Fresno: that somehow, the church we planted from scratch would become so trusted, so present, and so impactful that the people of our city, both inside and outside our congregation, would see it as essential as first responders.

That dream felt far off in those early days. And after we lost the opportunity to operate the $22million housing project, a loss that felt deeply personal, it was hard not to wonder if that dream had died.

> # DON'T DABBLE IN OUTREACH—DIVE IN.
> # DON'T TIPTOE AROUND BROKENNESS—RUN TO IT.

But then came our eighteenth-year anniversary celebration. We invited the mayor of Fresno to join us that day. He had always supported our involvement in the housing project, and his willingness to attend meant more to me than I can say. Just his presence was an encouragement, especially in a season where disappointment still lingered.

As he took the stage to speak, he began thanking our church for the tangible ways we served the city, especially how our team had fed thousands in the community. And then he said something I'll never forget:

"If Fresno had more churches like LifeBridge Community Church, we wouldn't even need a police department."

In that moment, as I held up my phone to record his words, I broke down. I sobbed—almost uncontrollably. I'll admit that I was a little embarrassed because I was overtaken with emotion.

But I was also overwhelmed with gratitude.

That dream from eighteen years ago—to become a church regarded with the same importance as our first responders—the one that felt impossible, the one that nearly slipped through our fingers, had come to life. We weren't the biggest church in town. We didn't have the flashiest building or the biggest budget. But we had something that mattered more: trust, faithfulness, and a mission that runs to the brokenness.

We were doing exactly what God called us to do: impacting people spiritually, socially, and economically.

Maybe the church needs to rethink its metrics of success. Maybe it's not so much about attendance charts or square footage or social media stats. Maybe success is simply this: obeying what God has uniquely called your church to do and doing it with everything you've got because the only metric that matters when we arrive in heaven one day is whether we did what our Master wanted us to do. Perhaps, as leaders, we should focus on that one moment instead of comparing our metrics with others.

 **GOD HAS MORE WAYS TO FUND HIS MISSION THAN WE CAN IMAGINE.**

When you simply focus on running to the brokenness, when you love your city without strings attached and serve it without needing recognition, you just might find that the dream God gave you is coming to life, one miracle at a time.

Pastor, I want you to hear this from me, not just as an author but as someone who has walked in your shoes:

I know what it's like to have more vision than budget.

I know what it's like to lie awake at night wondering how you'll cover payroll, fix the roof, or fund that outreach you know could change lives.

I know what it's like to watch dreams stall because the resources just aren't there.

It's frustrating. It's exhausting. And yes—it sucks.

But here's what I've learned: God has more ways to fund His mission than we can imagine. Sometimes, we just have to lift our heads, look beyond the offering plate, and trust Him to open new doors.

Also, remember this. We have the Holy Spirit inside of us. The same Spirit present at creation is present in you. You are filled with heaven's creativity. Lean into it.

You've got this. And you're not running alone.

If God can use an "average Joe" like me, He can use you. If He can use a church like ours, He can use yours.

I'm praying this final chapter gives you hope, practical ideas, and permission to dream again. You don't have to settle for survival. You can build a ministry that thrives—spiritually, socially, and economically—and that doesn't depend on whether next Sunday's giving is up or down.

Pastor, you are not alone. You are seen. And you are called for this moment.

Let's go build something beautiful—together.

NEXT STEPS

As you finish this book, I want to encourage you not to just be inspired but equipped. It's one thing to catch the vision, but it's another to build systems, culture, and leadership teams that make it sustainable for years to come. And I would love to journey with you, to cheer you on as you run to the brokenness in your city, as you help your people rise to meet the needs of your community, and as you become part of the unstoppable, global, redemptive mission of Jesus.

That's why I'm launching a coaching and consulting network for pastors and ministry leaders who want to lead their churches to become hubs of healing, hope, and transformation in their communities.

If your church wants to:
- Identify and meet the needs of your neighborhood
- Develop multiple streams of income to fund the mission
- Build a culture of outreach and compassion
- Equip leaders and volunteers to step into broken places

... I would love to walk alongside you.

We're building a movement of "Run to the Brokenness" churches—and you are invited.

(We'll include a section at the end of the book or a resources page where people can sign up or learn more.)

Let's go!

A PRAYER FOR PASTORS

Father,
I lift up every pastor and ministry leader reading these words. You see their heart. You know their burdens, their dreams, their frustrations, and their hopes.
Holy Spirit, remind them today that they are not alone. You are the same Spirit who hovered over the waters at creation, the same Spirit who brings creativity, wisdom, and power into our lives today. Fill them afresh. Give them divine ideas. Help them see new ways to reach their community and fund the mission You've placed in their hands.
Lord, I pray for supernatural provision over their lives and their churches. Open doors that no man can shut. Send people, resources, and opportunities from unexpected places. Give them the courage to step out in faith, the perseverance to keep going, and the joy of seeing lives transformed.
May they lead with integrity, vision, and passion, and may their churches shine as bright beacons of hope in their communities.
In Jesus's name,
Amen.

APPLICATION

- Schedule a meeting with your leadership team to discuss this vision.
- Identify one or two local needs you can begin addressing in the next thirty days.
- Begin a prayer initiative asking God to break your heart for what breaks His.

- Consider signing up for our Run to the Brokenness Church Network to get coaching, resources, and tools for your next steps.

REFLECTION

1) What are the biggest needs or areas of brokenness in your community right now?
2) In what ways do you currently feel "average" or underqualified, and how could that actually position you for God to use you?
3) When you think back to the moment God first called you, what comes to mind? How can remembering that calling strengthen you today?
4) Who are the key people or teams in your church that you need to bring together to cast vision for running to the brokenness?
5) How could partnering with a coaching or consulting network help your church take practical next steps toward becoming a "Run to the Brokenness" church?

RESOURCES FOR PASTORS AND LEADERS

Official Website
www.runtothebrokenness.com

Visit the official *Run to the Brokenness* website to access expanded tools and resources designed to help churches, leaders, and teams move from inspiration to implementation, including:

- Interactive Study Guide
- Church Campaign Kit
- Six Powerful Sermon Outlines
- Small Group Curriculum
- Compassion Activity Guide
- Church Readiness Assessment

RUN TO THE BROKENNESS

Available Resources
- Digital Video Masterclass
- eBook Edition
- Physical Study Guide
- Audiobook — Available on Audible, and on the website

Pastor Bundle
A comprehensive leadership package created specifically for pastors and ministry teams, including:
- Digital Video Masterclass
- eBook
- Digital Study Guide

ADDITIONAL TRUSTED RESOURCES

CITYSERVE
- A national movement equipping churches and nonprofits to serve communities through compassion initiatives.
www.cityservenetwork.com

CONVOY OF HOPE
- A faith-based humanitarian organization providing disaster relief, food distribution, and community outreach worldwide.
www.convoyofhope.org

TRUE INC.
- Grant and contract consultants helping organizations secure funding to expand community impact.
www.true.inc

NEIGHBORHOOD TO NATIONS
- A national grant center serving churches and nonprofits with training and access to funding opportunities.
www.ntngc.org

LISTEN WHEREVER YOU GET YOUR PODCASTS
AVAIL LEADERSHIP PODCAST

www.ingramcontent.com/pod-product-compliance
Lightning Source LLC
Chambersburg PA
CBHW070536090426
42735CB00013B/2995